Dragon WORRIERS

STORIES, WORKSHEETS, & THERAPEUTIC TOOLS TO OVERCOME CHILDHOOD ANXIETY

Dawn DePasquale, MA, LMHC

Published by
PESI Publishing & Media
PESI, Inc.
3839 White Ave
Eau Claire, WI 54703

Illustrations: Dawn DePasquale
Cover Design: Amy Rubenzer
Layout: Bookmasters & Amy Rubenzer

Proudly printed in the United States of America

ISBN: 9781683731863

PESI
Publishing
& Media
pesipublishing.com

About the Author

Dawn DePasquale is a Licensed Mental Health Counselor (LMHC) with a Master's degree in Clinical Psychology through the University of Massachusetts at Dartmouth, a program approved by the American Psychological Association (APA). She has worked in the mental health field since 2000, and her training and experience include one-on-one treatment as well as family, couples, and group therapy with both children and adults. Her focus is on the wellness of the entire person, not just the "presenting problem." Her passion for life and helping ease the pain of others has allowed her to work with amazing groups of people, helping them realize their dreams and begin loving their lives again.

Anyone can give you therapy, but can someone actually help you to really learn to love your life again? That's exactly what Dawn DePasquale does every day with her clinical team as the founder, CEO, and Clinical Director of Bell Mental Health Associates. Her personal philosophy is that everyone is an individual needing specific care tailored to their current needs, wants, and hopes. As part of her ongoing campaign to end the stigma of mental health disorder, Dawn carefully cultivates an environment of safety and ease within her clinic and is passionate about her work in the community, providing free mental health seminars regularly. She also volunteers her time as a mental health expert for local and internet radio and composes several blogs. She recently began writing *Ask Dawn*, a mental health advice blog for Southcoasttoday.com, in addition to her other blog containing mental health tips, *The Comfy Couch*. She was also a contributor to the international bestseller, *Share Your Message With the World*, and has recently begun work on the *Ginger Ninja* storybook series.

When not saving the world from the crushing specter of mental health issues, Dawn is active in the community as a teacher and activist. Her favorite job is being the doting mother of a spitfire daughter named Layla and reading vociferous amounts of comic books.

Dedication

This workbook is dedicated to my own little dragon, Layla, and to all of the little dragons I have had the pleasure of getting to know during my practice. Long live Longwei!

Table of Contents

How To Use This Book!

As a therapist, I have had the infinite pleasure of working with hundreds of lovely children and I can tell you one thing: universally, kids don't enjoy anxiety treatment. It's booooring. It's not fun. And worst of all? It feels like school! Too much work! I wanted to create a book that children would enjoy using, and thus, *Dragon Worriers* was born.

Each dragon character I've created experiences an anxiety disorder, allowing the child to relate to the character and learn from them. Through the different dragon stories and worksheets, children will see how anxiety can be a powerful tool in their life, and that they can also overcome problematic symptoms so they can have a happier, less anxious life.

Use this book in therapy, in the classroom, or at home—there's no wrong way, or wrong place to use it.

Here's How It Works:

First, it's important for you (the therapist, educator or caregiver) to explore the entire book. Check out the helper sections, the worksheets, tips, sample treatment plans, and the dragons to get a better idea of how you'd like to use this book.

When you're ready to use this book with a child, it's a good idea to start at Chapter 1. This chapter will introduce the child to the different dragons and will encourage some discussion about each one. Then, spend time with Chapters 2-4 to teach kids what anxiety feels like in their body, how to overcome anxious thoughts and how to make anxiety a superpower!

While reading Chapter 1, you may ask the child if they identify with something the different dragons are facing, and if they would like to learn more about them. If they do—jackpot! Go to that chapter (listed in the table of contents). At the beginning of each chapter is an engaging story with illustrations.

If the child isn't sure, or you're dealing with a child who is a bit worried or has some anxiety, but nothing specific, start with generalized anxiety disorder in Chapter 5.

Feel free to have fun and creatively use this book. Encourage the child to draw, color, write, and express themselves however they wish as they interact with the dragons.

Helper Sections:

These are the pages with squiggly borders! The helper sections include clinical information, such as how anxiety disorders are diagnosed, as well as hands-on information, like how a disorder may develop or how it may progress.

- If you're a clinician, treatment plans are included, as well as worksheets and case studies to help illustrate the course of treatment.

- For caregivers, you will find all sorts of information to help you to support your little one as they navigate the stormy waters of anxiety.

One More Hint:

This book features the villainous Ember, a mischievous dragon who feeds into the anxiety that the other dragons are feeling and makes everything worse! Encourage your child not only to recognize Ember throughout the book, but also to be on the lookout for the "Embers" in their lives that stir up anxious feelings. Forewarned is forearmed, and we want our kids to be able to protect themselves from their worries, even when we can't be right there to defend them. I always remind kids: we can't control the world, but we can control ourselves and give ourselves a chance to be our best selves. We can all be brave dragons!

And Thank YOU!

Have fun with this book! Being able to share these dragons' stories has been an amazingly blessed experience, and I hope this book will help to create peaceful minds and bodies for your little ones. Please feel free to share your experiences with me on my website at www.dawndepasquale.com or tweet me at Ninjatherapist7.

For courage, kindness, integrity and knowledge: Long live Longwei!

MEET THE DRAGON WORRIERS

Welcome, little traveler! My name is Abernaki, but you can call me "Abbie."

I am a dragon! What are you? A HUMAN?!?!? I am so excited to meet you! I haven't seen a human in such a long time! We don't get many visitors here in the Village of Longwei. You say it like this: "Looong way."

What brings you here? And speaking of here, on the next page is a map of our village. It may be helpful as you explore.

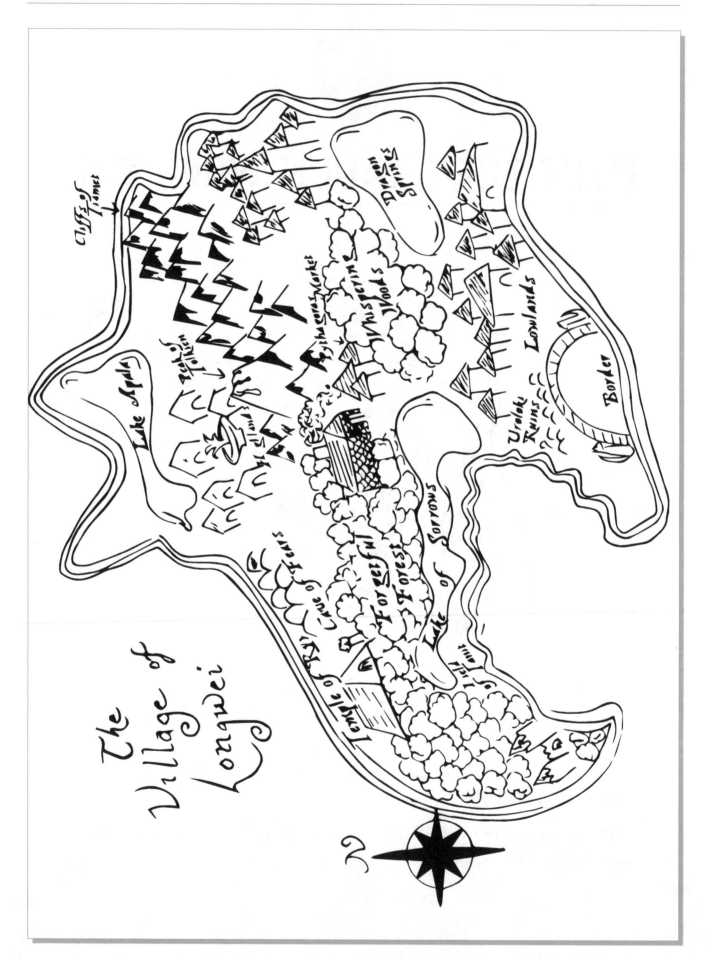

I know what you're thinking: Why haven't I ever heard of this place before? That's because the village is cloaked by magic: It is invisible to the naked eye! You may have never even seen a dragon before! However, things weren't always this way. Long ago, the dragon warriors lived in harmony with other creatures of the world.

They helped keep homes warm and they used their great wings to deliver food and supplies to villages across the globe.

They were well known for their recipes, which were flavored with dragon magic to create the most scrumptious foods!

They were known as brave, trustworthy friends who were always honest and truthful.

They enjoyed trick-or-treating with their friends and celebrating birthdays and all was right with the world.

But then one day a great illness befell the earth, making many sick. This may not seem like a big deal to you, perhaps you have had a cold before.

But the dragons had never been sick before. And do you know what happens when dragons get sick? They cough and they sniffle, and most of all, they sneeze!

When a dragon sneezes, he sometimes breathes fire. So, before they knew what was going on, the dragons had inexplicably set fire to their homes, the farmlands, and all of the surrounding areas.

Now the other people and creatures were understandably scared and upset, and they demanded that the dragons be rounded up and controlled.

The quick-thinking dragon General Adalinda the Noble rounded up whatever dragons she could and guided them to the icy waters of Lake Alpala, where they hid in its murky depths while all the other dragons were captured. When they were sure that the threat had passed, they used their magic to hide their new home from outsiders. This is why every Third of May we celebrate General Adalinda the Noble's Day by eating marshmallows and flying as high as we can to celebrate our freedom.

Now that they had a new home, the dragons had time to think about what had happened and how their lives had changed so much. Some of them became very upset and were concerned that they might be discovered and removed from the village. Still others couldn't shake a sense of dread that something awful might happen to them for no reason at all. **And just like that, the Dragon Warriors became the Dragon Worriers!**

But, listen to me, just gabbing along. Tell me a little bit about yourself!

ALL ABOUT ME!

My name: _Abernaki the Kind, but you can call me "Abbie"_

My age: _357 years old (still a youngling!)_

My favorite toy is: _My stuffed monkey, Max_

My favorite food is: _Spaghetti with meatballs – Yum!_

My favorite color is: _Blue_

My favorite thing to do is: _Exploring and meeting new friends_

Draw a picture of yourself!

ALL ABOUT ME!

My name: _____

My age: _____

My favorite toy is: _____

My favorite food is: _____

My favorite color is : _____

My favorite thing to do is: _____

Draw a picture of yourself!

Our village is named "Longwei," which means "Dragon Greatness," and our gates bear our town seal. Our town motto is "Courage, kindness, integrity, and knowledge": These are all traits that we dragons strive to maintain. We believe that with these skills, you can accomplish great things! Let me introduce you to some of the more colorful residents of our village.

This is General Uther Pendragon, our current leader. Most of us refer to him simply as "the General." He was pretty young when Longwei was first established, and he finds that he tends to worry—A LOT. It got so bad, we named a whole disorder after him: generalized anxiety disorder. It really interferes with his ability to get through his day sometimes. You will learn more about him in Chapter 5, and see ways that he is trying to handle his worries better.

The General

Duplos

Have you ever seen a two-headed dragon before? No? Well, that's not all that surprising. Dup and Los (known as Duplos together) come from a very rare species of dragon, the kind that typically have two heads, but could even have up to 10 or more! You've probably heard the saying, "Two heads are better than one," but Duplos would disagree with you.

What would you do if you had a second head, and it was always fighting with you? The problem is that one head is always thinking emotionally and the other only thinks in terms of rationality. You can read more about Dup and Los and how they learn to balance out emotions with rational thoughts in Chapter 6 by learning something called Dialectical Behavioral Therapy, or DBT.

Jumpy

See Jumpy here? He is really panicky! It all started... well, you'll see in Chapter 7. His worries are really getting the best of him. He has trouble sleeping, and he can't concentrate. Maybe we can help him learn to calm down and get past his panic disorder.

Good heavens! Look at poor Phobos! He is just running all over the place, afraid of his own shadow. He has a problem with severe fears, which we call phobias after our scared friend here. In Chapter 8 we will learn more about Phobos, and how to handle fears that just won't go away.

Phobos

Weepy

Have you ever missed someone you love, like *really* missed them, to the point it was hard to eat or sleep? Dear Weepy knows just how you feel. Weepy just started preschool and is having a lot of trouble being away from her parents and is experiencing something called separation anxiety. You will meet her in Chapter 9.

See that sweet little guy there? That is Monos, and you wouldn't know it from looking at him now, but he used to be the star of his school! But then things didn't quite go his way, and now he keeps to himself and stays far, far away from everyone. In Chapter 10 you will learn all about his social anxiety, and how he learned to get past it.

Monos

Mutos

This lovely youngling is Mutos, and you'll never hear a peep out of her. She is what you call selectively mute: She doesn't say a word. But she wasn't always that way: She was cursed! In Chapter 11 you will hear the exciting tale of how she lost her voice and then found it again!

Have you ever had something upsetting happen to you, and then you couldn't stop thinking about it? Woe knows exactly how you feel. He feels like when bad things happen it's like watching a movie rewind itself over and over again, as if it just keeps happening. This is called post-traumatic stress disorder, or PTSD for short. You will learn all about him and his friends in Chapter 12.

Woe

Rerun

Take a look at poor Rerun: Her head is on fire! That's because her brain is driving her crazy! She feels like she has to do all sorts of things *exactly right* so that more bad things won't happen. It's ruining her life! But all is not lost. With a little help from her dear Nana, she will be able to manage her thoughts and get rid of her obsessive-compulsive disorder. You can help out Rerun in Chapter 13.

Uh-oh, look who it is! Old Ember is back up to his tricks. You will find him throughout the book, as he tends to cause trouble in Longwei. Nobody knows for sure why, but he seems to delight in causing confusion and difficulty for our residents. In Chapter 14, we will go over some tips and tricks to avoid Ember, who tends to increase worries.

Ember

Chapter 2

FEELING ANXIETY IN YOUR BODY

Have you heard the story of Fainting Frannie and the Magic Breath? It is a really fun story! So here we go!

The Tale of Fainting Frannie and the Magic Breath

Fainting Frannie was such a goof off! Her friends always laughed whenever she got upset, because she would tremble and pass out. Even Frannie laughed about it sometimes. But other times... well, she felt like she was always on a roller coaster, dropping down, down, down, but never getting back up.

Her friends joked they could never throw her a surprise party, because old fainting Frannie would just drop like a ton of bricks the second they shouted "Surprise!"

One day at lunch, Frannie had a particularly scary fright and found herself waking up on the floor.

She looked into the kind face of Doctor Prudens. "My goodness, Frannie, you gave us quite a fright!" exclaimed the doctor. "What happened?"

Frannie tried to explain that sometimes when she feels very nervous or scared, she ends up waking up on the floor. "I'm broken, and I don't know what is wrong with me," Frannie said tearfully.

Now Doctor Prudens is a pretty smart fellow, and he thought he had a pretty good idea about what was happening. He explained that what she was experiencing was normal for all creatures, great and small. It is a way to stay safe.

"Every creature has something called a nervous system, and it helps us to stay safe. Yours is just stuck on too high a setting."

The doctor explained that even a small rabbit has a system that warns it when it might be in danger. Once it knows that there may be trouble, it has two options: fight, or flight. Once the body decides it needs to act, the brain will get the entire system moving in order to care for it.

The doctor broke it down simply:

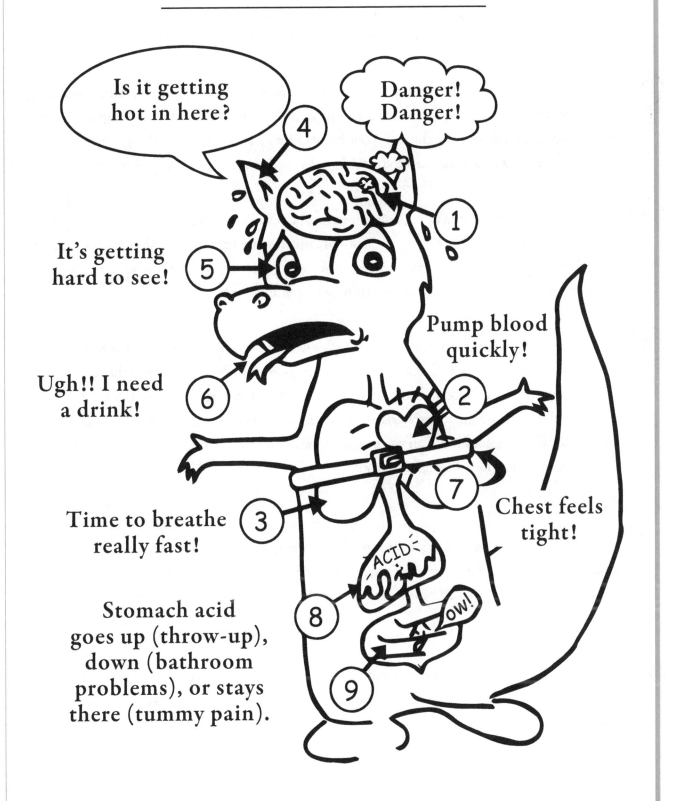

"Here is what happens when your body thinks you are in danger," Dr. Prudens began.

(1) All of your anxious thoughts start in your brain. Your brain thinks you are in danger, and the danger can be real or imaginary, it doesn't matter. Your fear is automatic. So the brain thinks you need to get to safety, and it immediately starts to activate different parts of your body.

(2) The first thing the brain activates is your heart. If you need to get away quickly from something dangerous, your muscles need to be warmed up. To do so, your heart starts to pump harder and faster, sending blood coursing through your body quickly. This does a few things: It can make your temperature go up, it can make your skin itchy, and it can even make you break out in a rash!

(3) To keep your heart pumping faster, your lungs need to change the way they are breathing. You know how when you are running you start to breathe faster and faster? Well, that's the same exact thing that happens when your brain tells your body to get to safety. Your lungs start to breathe faster and faster, and this allows your heart to keep pumping quickly.

(4) Remember how we said that the heart pumping fast sends blood coursing through the body? Well, in some spots it gets a little stuck. Your ears are a good example of this. When they feel the pressure from all of that blood moving quickly, your ears have more trouble hearing. Sometimes, it might feel like you are dizzy, or sounds may be muffled. It will be harder to tell where sound is, something called echolocation. Can you imagine how crummy that feels, not being able to hear right and then feeling like you might pass out?

(5) As if that's not enough, your eyes are affected, too. We have a weird biological impulse that kicks in when it thinks we are in danger. Your field of vision gets smaller, so you can easily find your way to safety without being distracted by other items in the area. This might make you feel like the walls are closing in, or that there is a darkness on the sides of your vision. It feels like the lights are going out!

(6) At this point, you have air coming in and out of your body quickly, and your temperature has gone up. That means your mouth will get dry and your tongue may even swell slightly, making it harder to talk.

(7) See the belt here? That's not a real belt, but it symbolizes how your chest may feel very tight the faster and faster you breathe. It might also feel like there is a heavy weight on your chest, making it harder and harder for you to breathe.

(8) Now comes the grand finale: your stomach. Your body figures that at this point you probably need to run away. It's hard to run with a bunch of food in your stomach, so your stomach will start to release acid to help break down any food hanging out in there. This is fine, if you have a bunch of pasta or something in there. But if not, stomach acid has to go to one of three places. First, it can go up, leading to nausea and acid reflux or burping. It could also go down, leading to stomach disturbance and diarrhea. Or, it could simply stay in your stomach where it can really do some damage! It can burn a hole there, something we doctors call an ulcer. That requires special medicine and is really uncomfortable!

(9) As you can imagine, this might lead to you feeling like you have to go to the bathroom *a lot*. And let's face it, if you are spending all of your time in the bathroom, you're not going to have much time to enjoy the rest of your life.

"So, Frannie," asked Doctor Prudens, "Where does your body feel upset when you get anxious?"

Frannie really thought hard about when she is upset. Then it came to her!

When she started to feel worried, she noticed she first felt warm, like the room had suddenly caught fire!

"So what do I do about it?" Frannie asked.

"Well, that's simple," the doctor said. "Your body is an engine, so in order to slow an engine down, you have to decrease its power source.

Your heart can only pump fast if your breath is fast as well. If you make your breath slow and controlled, your heart will follow. Think of it like blowing bubbles. In order to get nice, big bubbles, you need slow and controlled air. Let's try it together."

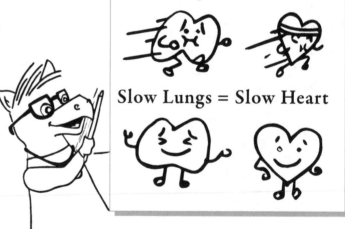

Fast Lungs = Fast Heart

Slow Lungs = Slow Heart

Doctor Prudens took out some bubble solution and offered it to Frannie. She took a nice, slow breath, and then worked on blowing as many bubbles as big as she could, all with slow, controlled breaths.

Frannie was amazed that when she breathed slower, she did feel calmer. The doctor checked her heart beat and then let her listen, too. Like magic, Frannie's heart was slowing down and she was starting to feel better. It was amazing!

Doctor Prudens explained that Frannie can always breathe, even when she is upset. He suggested that she should practice breathing nice and deep and slow when she *isn't* upset so she will be able to control her breathing better when she is upset. He explained that the more she practices, the more she will be able to calm herself and feel better. They talked about music that Frannie finds soothing and she agreed to practice breathing every day for three minutes to some songs she enjoys.

Doctor Prudens explained that when Frannie allows herself to breathe deeply, it is like giving her body a gift. It calms her down and helps her to think more clearly. He also suggested that she find things she enjoys doing and make a point of doing them regularly in order to encourage her body to relax more easily. Frannie thanked the doctor happily. She was feeling better already!

Once she returned home, Frannie tried to figure out what she could do to calm her body down. Her mom suggested she find something she already enjoys and spend time doing that. Frannie loved going for long walks in the woods and her mom suggested she take her walks and look—really look—at her surroundings.

"Smell every smell! See every sight!" her mother suggested.

Frannie made it a point to go on walks as often as she could and to take nice, deep breaths when she did. Soon, she started to notice that she was walking with a skip in her step, and she was feeling less nervous all the time.

Fainting Frannie soon lost her nickname. Now her friends all call her Fun-loving Frannie, because she is so happy all the time, and not just because things are good around her but because she *chooses* to be happy! Now she helps others to calm their bodies, too!

Neat story, right? Our bodies really are amazing! They tell us all sorts of things, and they are really helpful when it comes to keeping us safe. Sometimes when we don't listen to our bodies they have to get louder and louder, until we might feel like we can't even tell what the body is saying anymore. But if we start to really listen to our bodies, not just when they are upset but all of the time, they make music that is truly beautiful.

How does your body talk to you? It's important we listen to its messages so we can stay safe and feel well. If you were sneezing and felt sick, you'd go to bed, right? That's exactly what I'm talking about. If your body is telling you there might be a problem, it's a good idea to find out what's going on so you can make good choices. It's a good idea to check in with your body from time to time to make sure that you are listening to it accurately.

Ask yourself: Where is my body talking? Find the spot on your body and feel it with your hands, your mind, or your heart. Now ask, what is my body saying? It might say something like, "Be careful!" or "I'm in trouble!" or even "Do they like me?" It's okay if you don't know for sure, just keep listening.

Now look around. Is there anything that is actually putting you in danger? Sometimes we see something and think about it so quickly, we might *feel* there is a problem but not really understand or fully notice it. Give the area a quick scan and ask yourself:

Is there something here that makes me feel worried or afraid?

Am I predicting that something bad might happen?

Am I in any actual danger that I know of?

It's okay to feel worried, even if you cannot figure out why. But if you see that you are not in danger, it makes sense to let yourself relax a little. Thank your body for being so helpful, and take a nice, deep breath. Your body loves to breathe!

THINGS I LIKE TO DO!

Now that you and your body had a nice chat, it's a good idea to make sure that you are taking good care of your body for all of the good things it does for you. What types of things does your body like to do? Let's make a list!

MY FAVORITE FOODS

Taking care of your body means you need to give it good food so it can work properly. Think of your body like a car. A car runs best when it has the best fuel. Let's draw some pictures of your favorite foods!

Draw a picture of yourself eating your favorite foods and how you feel when you are enjoying them!

MY GOODNIGHT CHECKLIST

Rest is also important for your body. I know little dragons don't necessarily like to sleep, but it is important. What do you need to help you get your best sleep? I like a nightlight, do you? Here is a checklist of things that can help you sleep. If you review these with an adult, they can help you if you are not sleeping well.

My bedtime is: _____

One hour before bedtime:
- ❑ No exercise or loud playing
- ❑ Dim the lights in your house
- ❑ Avoid sugary snacks

Half an hour before bed:
- ❑ Raise your body temperature by taking a hot bath or shower, or drink a warm beverage (non-caffeinated)
- ❑ Put on some comfortable pajamas
- ❑ Turn on your nightlight (if you're using one)
- ❑ Get comfy in your bed and say your good nights
- ❑ DO NOT use any electrical devices, like tablets, cell phones, or computers (they keep you awake)
- ❑ It's best not to watch television before bed (and NOT to have a television in your bedroom) but if you must watch TV, watch something soothing and put a sleep timer on so that that it turns off within an hour
- ❑ Use a sound machine if you need ambient noise

If you are having trouble sleeping:
- ❑ Try reading a book
- ❑ Listen to calming music
- ❑ Take deep breaths
- ❑ Say prayers or meditate
- ❑ If you are hungry, have a small, non-sugary snack. It's hard to sleep on an empty stomach. Crackers and cheese are a good idea!

Remember, if you take good care of your body, it will take good care of you!

Anxiety and the Body

In this chapter, we are introducing children to the idea of how the body works in order to help them gain a more thorough understanding of how anxiety impacts their bodies and allow them to interpret their symptoms in order to manage their anxiety better. Knowing what their first symptoms are helps children to understand when to use their skills. A treatment tool will be utterly ineffective if it is used at the wrong time, so you need to teach children early on when their body is starting to feel anxious so they can calm themselves before they are thrown into a full-blown panic attack.

Some clinicians worry that teaching children about the mechanics of the body will be overwhelming: I think the opposite is true. I think knowledge is power, and teaching a child how his or her body responds to anxiety is a powerful tool in their recovery arsenal.

When I teach children about anxiety, I draw it out for them so they can be mindful of each part of the body and give me feedback about how the different parts work together. Think of it like this: When the child is experiencing abject anxiety, he or she may be far away from anyone who can guide them through the relaxation process. They have to rely on *themselves* to know they are experiencing anxiety and then be able to manage it. The sooner you teach them these skills, the better.

It's important that you review the physical symptoms of anxiety with any caregivers who work with the child as well, as they need to support these children while they grow in this process. Some people view anxiety as a flaw or an imaginary fear. By reviewing how the body works, you help caregivers and their children to understand that fear is a normal bodily response, and that because children are young and don't understand how the world works they are more prone to fantastical thoughts that lead to anxiety. Anxiety is all about feeling. In anxiety, what you feel is real; it becomes your reality. This is why your primary defense will be ongoing education and reality-testing to help the children you work with to manage their worries in controlled, healthy ways. Go, you!

On the following page is a quick handout I use with parents when working on anxiety.

ANXIETY AWARENESS INFORMATION SHEET

Anxiety is a response of the central nervous system to a perceived danger. Anxiety becomes a clinical disorder when it results in ongoing worry, even when there is no clear danger present. There are many different types of anxiety, but the symptoms of an anxiety disorder can include:

- Restlessness or feeling wound-up or on edge
- Being easily fatigued
- Difficulty concentrating or having their minds go blank
- Irritability
- Muscle tension
- Difficulty controlling the worry
- Sleep problems (difficulty falling or staying asleep, or restless, unsatisfying sleep)

What does it feel like?

When you experience anxiety, your body goes through a complex set of reactions designed to keep you safe from harm. In a nutshell, here is what your body does when it is anxious:

1. Your heart beats faster to get blood to your extremities.

2. In order for your heart to beat faster, your lungs breathe shallowly.

3. Your temperature raises when your heart rate increases, causing you to sweat.

4. Your skin may become itchy or you may break out in hives because of the release of cortisol from your adrenal glands when your heartbeat increases.

5. Your hearing becomes muffled because of the sudden influx of blood to the ears. Additionally, your balance may be thrown off or you may feel dizzy.

6. Your pupils will dilate, making it feel like the walls are closing in.

7. Your mouth will become dry and you may have some post-nasal drip, causing you to have to clear your throat repeatedly.

8. Your chest will tighten as your breath becomes more forced and shallow.

9. Your stomach will release acid in order to get rid of any food inside. Stomach acid will either rise, causing you to feel nauseous or throw up; it will go into your intestines, making you experience diarrhea; or it will stay in your stomach, which can cause significant damage and create a hole called an ulcer in the stomach lining.

It is important to note that all creatures have anxiety, because every living thing has a central nervous system to keep it safe. That means all people should, in fact, become nervous at times. And it's not all bad! Anxiety helps us to get to work on time, and to avoid burning ourselves on hot pans. Please be aware that this reaction can become overwrought when it is happening too often, or when people around the child are demonstrating negative reactions to stress. For an example, if your mom handled the power going out by crying in the corner, you might think this is how an adult should handle stress. Be a strong power of example! Explore your own patterns of stress management and make sure you are giving your child a positive role model for anxiety.

Remember that when you are stressed you are more likely to develop and indulge in bad habits. This means you need to take good care of yourself and engage in appropriate stress management regularly. Your body and your child will thank you, because a calm parent is a good parent.

Finally, the most important thing in early anxiety work is to help normalize the experience of anxiety and to work on breathing. Breathing is key in relaxing the body and helping the child feel control over their bodies. Feel free to guide your child through the handouts listed in the children's section of this chapter to create a great base to begin managing not only the current anxiety but any new anxiety that might rear its ugly head!

Unbeknownst to them, Captius was going to the place he always goes when he is upset: The old abandoned treehouse in the Forgetful Forest.

He went there sometimes just to think, or to try out some new ideas. What he had never told anyone was he sometimes went there to escape his thoughts. He would pretend his awful, bad thoughts about himself couldn't get into the treehouse. He *needed* to be perfect, and it was getting harder and harder to do it. He worried about getting sick, because he thought if he missed school he would fall behind and fail. And if he failed, he would let everyone down: his teachers, his friends, his family. If he let his family down, how could they love him anymore? Could they love a loser like him? Surely not.

And now his worst worries were coming true: He was going to fail. They would abandon him, and he would be all alone. Unloved. Unwanted. He felt like he would never stop crying.

He heard a tap at the treehouse door. "Go away!" he snarled through his tears. But the tapping persisted. In walked the last person Captius expected to see.

"Why are you crying?" asked his sister, fearfully. She was clutching her little bunny.

Captius was so embarrassed he yelled at her again, but she would not leave. Instead, she started to cry, too. "I'm so sorry I messed up your project. I ruined everything! I am such a loser!"

"No, Annie! Don't say such terrible things. You are a great kid!" Captius said.

"No, I'm not! I am the worst sister ever! I will never be as smart as you or as perfect as you. Look at all of your trophies! I can't even get a trophy for participation! And then I go and ruin your project. I wouldn't blame you if you never *ever* spoke to me again."

Captius was shocked at what he was hearing. He tried so hard to be perfect, but that very thing made his sister feel bad about herself. Maybe because she never saw him mess up, she thought she couldn't either?

Captius hugged Annie tightly and explained that he overreacted about the incident with the science fair project. He explained he was very proud of her, and that winning trophies wasn't everything. There were so many things she did better than him, like doing cartwheels and skipping rope. She could blow bigger bubbles than him. And burp louder, too!

Captius wanted to make Annie feel better, and he had a great idea! "Why don't you try to teach me some of the stuff you do well, and I'll teach you some of the stuff I do well?"

"What about stuff neither of us do well?" Annie asked.

"Then we can both mess up together!" Captius said. "Wanna head back to the house?" And with that, the two walked back to the house, hand-in-hand.

Captius feels like he has to do everything right all the time—what an exhausting way to live! No one is perfect. In fact, it's our imperfections that make us special and wonderful. If we were all the same, what a boring world we would be in. What makes you special? Let's write it down!

WHAT MAKES YOU SPECIAL?

This is a really important question, because what makes you special makes you amazing! Sometimes it's hard to figure out what makes us different, so here are some great questions to help you out.

1. What is something you are talented at?

2. What is a nickname someone has given you?

3. What is something you would like to be when you grow up?

4. What is the name of something you love very much?

5. If you had to describe yourself in just two words, what would they be?

6. If you could have any superpower, what would it be?

Now, take all of these answers and draw a picture of yourself on a separate piece of paper. You are special!

Captius didn't realize how important his job of being a big brother was to his little sister. Sometimes we can get overwhelmed by the many roles we play in life. Here are the many roles Captius plays.

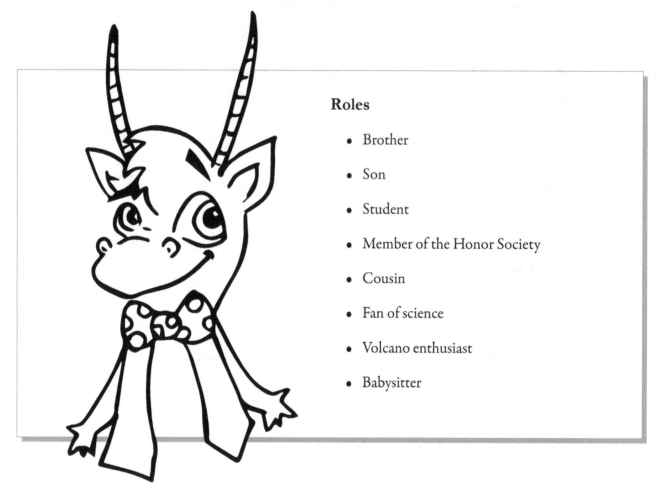

Roles

- Brother

- Son

- Student

- Member of the Honor Society

- Cousin

- Fan of science

- Volcano enthusiast

- Babysitter

What roles do you play? Are some of them more important to you than others? Do you like some more than others? It's important we know what roles we play in our lives and that they are appropriate for us. If we take on roles that are not appropriate, like Captius feeling like he has to be "always perfect," it can lead to us feeling overwhelmed and anxious. It's important to tell an adult you trust if you feel like you have a role in your life that is not right for you.

Finally, both Captius and Annie said some really crummy things about themselves. When we say mean things to ourselves, it's like we are being our own worst enemy. Why would you bully yourself? Let's help Captius think better things about himself. Can you help correct his bad thoughts into better, kinder thoughts?

THE GOOD THOUGHTS CONVERTER

So here is how it works. You put a bad thought into the converter, and it evaluates the thought to see if it is true or false. If it is true, it converts the thought to a kind thought. If it is false, it converts it to the truth. Here are a few examples:

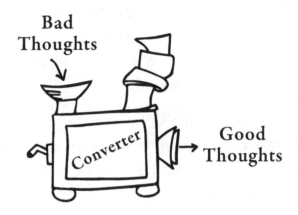

Thought	Converter	New Thought!
"I am SO stupid!"	You know it isn't true.	"I am smart. I just had a tough time today..."
"I was mean to my sister."	That is true, but not kind.	"I can apologize to her and I am not usually mean to her. I try to be a good brother!"

Now you try...

You need to be your own best friend! Remind yourself of what makes you special and correct those bad self-thoughts to help you feel better anytime you need a little boost. General Adalinda wisely once said, "No one moves forward without kindness," so give yourself kindness and you will be surprised at how much better you will feel!

Case Study: Misty

We opened this chapter by examining one of the personality types known to lead to higher amounts of anxiety: people who are designated as "Type A." Simply put, these are people who tend to be perfectionistic, competitive, highly organized. Let's examine a case study.

Misty came to me at the tender age of 12 years old. She was referred because she had started displaying severe emotional swings, especially in regard to her school work, which her teachers describe as "impeccable." Her parents were worried as she was sleeping and eating less than before.

I meet Misty on her way to basketball practice. She is involved in several after-school activities as well as some community activities. She volunteers at her church and she excels in school, insisting on taking the most difficult classes possible.

When I speak with Misty, I am initially taken aback by how carefully she speaks and her need for frequent reassurance. She has a high need for perfection and has a very low threshold of frustration tolerance, which isn't surprising given how naturally gifted she is. In fact, Misty excels in practically every single thing she tries. Unfortunately though, she's actually *too good*: Because she never fails, she never has to learn how to handle a failure. The idea of being rejected for any reason at all almost paralyzes her with fear. Her very identity hinges on being perfect and accomplishing anything put before her.

I let her know failure is an important part of life, as it teaches resilience. Anyone can fall down, I suggest. It's the ones who get back up we respect. Those are the ones who have integrity, the ones who have tenacity. Perfection never lasts, and if you fall apart at the first little problem, you will never move forward in your life. You might as well be a fainting goat! Instead, we have to learn how to overcome adversity.

I share with her the names of some well-known people who have overcome adversity, and how they initially may have been written off by their peers as useless, but they actually made a huge change in other people's lives. People like Thomas Edison, Walt Disney, and Beethoven. Edison was told he was "too stupid to learn anything" by a teacher early on in his life; Disney was told he had "no good ideas" by a publisher; Beethoven was told he would never be a composer. How wrong those critics were! They were able to accomplish anything they put their minds to, not because the task was easy but because they were *not*. They were made out of tougher stuff, they refused to give up. They picked a goal and they fought for it. That is something to be proud of!

With a kid like Misty, I am going to need to help her let go of her current perfectionist identity and instead embrace a better, more realistic and loving version of herself. I am going to start by building up her self-esteem. That means I need to help her to examine those negative self-thoughts, just like Captius did, and replace them with more realistic statements. I have her use The Good Thought Converter worksheet to focus on rewriting the negative commentary she gives herself. Then we are going to explore her likes and dislikes and her talents, as well as things she may not be good at or simply chooses not to do. We talk about the fact that just because she can do something doesn't mean she has to do it.

Our next step will be to work on creating realistic expectations in regard to what Misty can accomplish given her own skill set, the tools available to her, her individual level of interest, and the time she has available. We will then compare these to expectations she has for a similar peer.

I use the Creating Realistic Expectations worksheet on the following page with Misty.

Our goal is to help Misty become a well-adjusted person with dreams and hopes just like everyone else, but without that awful feeling you get when you push yourself too hard. I remind her that the point of our relationship with anyone, even ourselves, is to love them and to help them grow.

If we have a garden, we give it sunshine and water: We don't yell at it, thrash at it, and cut it off from the very things it needs to live. Kindness and love are like water to us. We need to spread them freely, even to ourselves, just like our loved ones do for us if we hope to grow up healthy and strong.

CREATING REALISTIC EXPECTATIONS

Expectation:

I will get straight A's in Spanish.

Do I have the skills I need to accomplish this goal? Why or why not?

I don't speak Spanish, so I have to learn everything new in class.

Do I have the tools I need to accomplish this goal? Why or why not?

I try to learn as much as I can in school, but sometimes I have to look up information on my own. I am learning Spanish, but I don't speak Spanish and no one else I know speaks Spanish.

Do I have the level of interest necessary to do this?

I try to learn as much as I can, but I don't like Spanish class and I don't know when I will use it in my town (we all speak English). I am not very interested in the language or the culture, and I don't think I will travel to any Spanish-speaking countries any time soon.

Do I have the time to accomplish this goal?

My Spanish homework takes up a lot of my time, and I have to work twice as hard at it as I do at the rest of my homework. Some days I barely finish before bed.

Would I expect someone else to accomplish this goal? Would I expect my best friend, my parent, or a stranger to accomplish this goal?

I would not expect my best friend, my Mom, or a stranger to get straight A's in Spanish unless they already spoke the language. That class is hard!

What conclusions can I draw from this? Is my expectation realistic or not? Can I get help with this expectation if I need it?

It doesn't make sense to think I will magically be able to speak Spanish when I have never spoken the language before. All I can do is my best. Because I don't enjoy the class, I might want to look into other options for next year. If I continue to struggle, I might want to get some extra help.

CREATING REALISTIC EXPECTATIONS

Expectation:

Do I have the skills I need to accomplish this goal? Why or why not?

Do I have the tools I need to accomplish this goal? Why or why not?

Do I have the level of interest necessary to do this?

Do I have the time to accomplish this goal?

Would I expect someone else to accomplish this goal? Would I expect my best friend, my parent, or a stranger to accomplish this goal?

What conclusions can I draw from this? Is my expectation realistic or not? Can I get help with this expectation if I need it?

Case Study: Paul

Another personality type that can lead to anxiety is the caregiver persona. This is a child who feels responsible for others and in so doing, loses sight of their own needs. If you have a child who loses themselves in caring for another, whether it be another child, an adult, or an animal, they are opening themselves up to exploitation and potential harm over time. They grow up too fast and miss the important lessons all children need to learn, lessons of friendship and hope.

Paul is brought into therapy by his grandfather, who has custody of the child. He is nine years old when I meet him. Paul was recently removed from his mother's custody following her (yet another) arrest for drug trafficking. Paul reports he has vivid memories of waking his mother up so she wouldn't overdose and forcing her to eat and drink "so she wouldn't die." He remembers living in apartments full of bugs and having people coming and going at all times of the day and night. People he was afraid of, but who he was told to be nice to regardless.

His mother is now in a treatment facility and Paul lies awake at night worried about her. Is she eating? Is she sleeping? Who will make sure she sees the doctor when she is supposed to? Who will make sure she is safe from the people who threatened her with guns in front of her own son? When I start working with Paul, I need to ally with him in regard to his feelings about his mother and help him to tell his story. I help him to normalize his experience and validate his feelings of trauma and fear. Eventually I will work on creating a better understanding in regard to the proper roles of children versus those of adults. I help him to understand what is expected of children as well as what is expected of adults. He will eventually see that in his relationship with his mother, *he* was the adult and *she* was the child.

We use the Expectations worksheet on the following page to help with this, as it opens up a conversation about what the child's expectations are and allows you to see where you need to start molding these thoughts into more appropriate ideas.

EXPECTATIONS: CHILDREN VERSUS ADULTS

For the following tasks, select who should do the task. If both an adult and child could do it, feel free to circle both.

Make dinner for others	Child	Adult
Tuck people in	Child	Adult
Buy groceries	Child	Adult
Take care of others when they are sick	Child	Adult
Play outside	Child	Adult
Go to school	Child	Adult
Earn money for the house	Child	Adult
Call and make a doctor's appointment	Child	Adult
Make mistakes	Child	Adult
Drive people places	Child	Adult
Buy a winter jacket	Child	Adult
Feed pets	Child	Adult

Add your own ideas here:

When Paul realizes he was more of a parent than his mother was, he experiences a significant period of sadness as he mourns his old identity of caregiver as well as some anger toward his mother for putting him into such an uncomfortable position. Paul explains to me that his mother had no right to make him her caregiver and that if she was better at caring for him, she would have placed him with a responsible adult while she tried to straighten her life out. He uses words like "selfish" and "childish" to describe her actions.

We work on separating who she is from what she has done and discuss how his mother has only a limited number of tools to be a good parent in her possession. We can't blame her for what she doesn't know, but we can expect that she try her hardest to care for her son, as this is the primary responsibility of any parent. We discuss the concept of "loving the sinner while hating the sin," as Paul is a devout Catholic since moving in with his grandfather.

I work with Paul on managing his anxiety through the Anxiety Log on the following pages.

ANXIETY LOG

Questions to ask yourself:	Your response:
Precisely what am I worried about?	
Exactly what am I predicting will happen?	
How likely (0 to 100%) do I feel this is going to happen?	
Am I predicting a catastrophe (something awful) that is unlikely to come true? If so, what catastrophe am I predicting?	
What is the evidence FOR this worry that something really bad is going to happen?	
What is the evidence AGAINST this worry that something really bad is going to happen?	
Is my evidence based mostly on logic or emotions? For example, am I thinking something awful must be happening because I feel upset?	
Have I ever been wrong in the past about my worries? What actually happened?	

What does it cost me to worry about this?	
What is the benefit of worrying about this?	
Has worrying ever been HELPFUL to me? How?	
Has worrying ever been HURTFUL to me? How?	
If what I worry about actually happens, what would be the realistic result?	
Am I underestimating my ability to handle the problem? How?	
How do I think I will feel about this situation I am worried about in a week, a month, a year? Would I feel differently? If so, why?	
If a good friend of mine was experiencing this worry, what would my advice be? Would I suggest that this person worry as much as I am?	

I also work with Paul on daily deep breathing, prayer as a form of meditation, and doing things he enjoys. He is great at Minecraft, so we agree 30 minutes of concentrated Minecraft play with friends is a good idea a few times a week as long as his school work is being done. He also takes up running and joins a recreational team at his school to explore his interest with like-minded friends. We want to create some positive supports to help him handle any upcoming negative events.

The next step is to help Paul normalize his life with his grandfather. Paul is used to doing many things that are inappropriate for a nine-year-old child. He doesn't understand that when his grandfather gives him a bedtime and wants him to eat his vegetables, this is his way of showing love and care for Paul. He thinks instead, "He's treating me like a baby" and, "He doesn't think I'm a man." We work on supporting Paul's feelings about his own identity and masculinity while marrying these with the appropriate identity of a child who is nine.

Something often forgotten when dealing with a caregiver child is that they can feel very isolated from others, as children of the same age typically will not share the same life experiences. Another issue is they may be more mature in some ways than their peers and this will make it harder for them to make friends. They may be less tolerant of age-appropriate behaviors because they spend most of their time interacting with adults.

This is another reason I encourage Paul to play online with friends and to engage in recreational activities with his peers. I work with him on learning to tolerate the behaviors of children his own age. He cannot understand why they are ill-mannered, or why they need so much guidance when he doesn't. He once came in and asked me in bewilderment, "What *is* their obsession with farts?" I almost fell off my chair! I explained to him that it is very normal for nine-year-olds to find bodily functions to be the epitome of humor. In many ways, I am his translator as he adjusts to his new life.

— Conclusion —

These case studies present some clear stressors, but it's important to be able to validate the child's experience of stress and to make it clear that the only thing necessary to create a stressful event is for it to be stressful to the bearer. It doesn't matter if other people find it stressful.

I let kids know their lives are very stressful, much more stressful than when I was their age. I am a child of the 80s. I spent a good portion of my time playing with She-Ra toys or pretending to be Madonna (the cool 80s one, not the creepy one we have now... brr!). I'm not sure if the world was as scary as it is today or if I just didn't know about it, but I definitely know I couldn't just tap a button and find out about horrible things happening all over the world. Further, if a kid didn't like me, maybe they'd give me the evil eye or worse yet, write something awful on the bathroom walls. They couldn't publicly embarrass me or get their 5,000 followers to support their opinion. They couldn't photoshop me into weird situations that were increasingly embarrassing. And when I was upset, I couldn't click a button and read about things that would terrify me until I couldn't sleep due to the nightmares they created.

Please be aware that anxious kids have a natural attraction to provocative media and experiences. Such events allow them to flex their adrenal glands and to release some of that pent-up tension. They feel a momentary sense of release. The problem is, the more they do it, the more they *want* to do it, and before they know it, they are constantly seeking out the stimuli. Some researchers have suggested this becomes a type of addiction.

I ask parents to monitor what their kids are watching, listening to, and doing. If they don't have parental controls on their devices, let's get those in place immediately. There are apps I suggest to monitor their child's web activity and send a daily report (pretty much every device has one). Is it more work for parents? Yes, but if you choose as a parent to allow your child access to billions of voices, both informed and uniformed, the least you can do is find out who they are listening to. Watch out for websites that offer scary thrills quickly and engage your child in a conversation about how this can lead to an increase in anxiety. Remember: Therapy doesn't just happen in the office, it needs to happen in the home as well. So we all need to help guide children throughout the real world; normalize their stressors and help them to find positive solutions to the many difficulties life can throw them. It's the best way to help them become the great people we know they can be.

Chapter 4

ANXIETY AS YOUR SUPERPOWER

Behold the legend of Super Dragon!

He is a superhero who protects all of the people in our village. He has many gifts, like super speed, super hearing, super sight, and speed reading. Okay, that last one's not really a superpower, but it does come in handy! His greatest power of all, though, is his ability to be aware of what's going on around him so that he can act accordingly to keep himself and others safe. That's a superpower a lot of people call "anxiety," but he calls it power! He can even use it to predict the future, which really comes in handy!

Super Dragon

Because Super Dragon has enhanced senses, he can tell when bad things are going to happen. That sounds pretty great, right? But Super Dragon didn't always feel so great about it.

Before he was called Super Dragon, SD was a little dragon just like you or me. But he was always a little bit... different.

But it didn't really cause him much concern until he started to get a little older. That's when he noticed some weird things happening. He noticed he could tell when something was going to happen, and he could hear sounds far away.

It was all very confusing for Super Dragon: Why was he hearing and seeing things other people couldn't? He didn't want to be different or stand out. He wanted to be just like everyone else. He started to get really worried about what might happen that he couldn't predict, and it kept him up at night.

On one night in particular, SD's dad came in to check on him and was surprised to see him still awake.

"What's the matter son?" SD's dad asked.

"I don't like being different," SD said, hiding his head.

"Being different is wonderful!" his dad said. "I love that you are different. In fact, I wouldn't want you to be any other way."

"But things are always coming at me. It's like I can feel everything that is going to happen, good and bad. I can't handle it. I'm not strong enough."

"Son," SD's dad began, "it's like taking a shower. When you take a shower all of the water comes at you. If you pay attention to every little drop of water, it would make you very upset. You would feel like you were being attacked. But it doesn't bother us, because we know this is what it is like to feel a shower on us, so we allow it. Did you know that your snout is always in the way when you look around, but your brain just ignores it because it knows that it is okay? We learn to tolerate things, and this helps us to feel less stressed out."

Super Dragon was amazed at this news!

"Super Dragon, you have an amazing power. You must use it for good. You alone can help others who need help! You can be the Super Dragon you were always intended to be. You can be a hero, but you have to be able to decide what is worthy of your attention and what is not. Will you hear the cry of your people and help them in their hour of need?"

And so Super Dragon was born! He agreed to use his powers for good, and now he can almost predict things before they are happening because he pays such close attention to everything around him. His anxiety is a blessing; it allows him to help a nice lady with her groceries, or to grab some ice cream before it hits the floor. He also can tell when his arch-nemesis, Doctor Doubt, is nearby.

That guy is always trying to trick Super Dragon into making bad choices! Super Dragon has learned that the best way to master doubt is to calm his mind, not let himself get overwhelmed with emotion, and to make the next right move!

YOU are a superhero, too! Just like Super Dragon, your enhanced senses tell you when things might be happening. I bet sometimes you make really good choices all by yourself, just because you rely on your superpowers to tell you what is going on and what to do next. Your anxiety is a superpower!

Let's create your new superhero identity! I did one, too, just to help you out!

I AM A SUPERHERO!

My new superhero name is: *Super Abbie!*

Here is what I look like in my superhero outfit:

These are ways my superpowers help me: *I can tell when I am scared and I can hear better and see better to keep myself safe! I can slow my heart down just by using my super breathing!*

I AM A SUPERHERO!

My new superhero name is:

Here is what I look like in my superhero outfit:

These are ways my superpowers help me:

Don't forget: You have an amazing, exciting, superpower! Anxiety is a blessing! With a little help, you can learn how to control it and use it for good!

The First Treatment Session

Let's talk about the first time a child meets with a therapist. It's pretty scary when you're a child and your parents get you all dressed up to meet a new person. It is likely that you are either in trouble or getting a shot! Anyone coming into a therapy meeting for the first time will be a little bit nervous, and children are no different. If you think about it, they have so little control over their lives at their age. People tell them when to sleep, when to wake, what to eat, where to go, what to wear... it's no wonder anxiety creeps into their minds when they feel they cannot control things.

When I first meet a child, I want them to know they do have some control when they are with me. When I meet them, I shake their hand and let them know I am interviewing for a job. Here is a sample script:

D: "Hi, I'm Dawn, and I am very excited to meet you today. What's your name?"

Pt: "Tommy."

D: "Tommy, it's great to meet you. I am hoping you will hire me. I had you come here today so I can see if you would let me work with you. I'm a special type of person who helps special people like yourself to feel as happy as they can. Let me show you my office."

Once the child is in the office, I encourage him or her to explore the space and to ask any questions they feel in the moment. Sometimes, parents will want to dive into the problem, but I find making the patient feel comfortable is important enough to delay this. I encourage kids to look around my office (it's not all that big) and to let me know if there is something they like or that gets their attention. I have a few stuffed animals I will tell children stories about if they ask.

Once the child has settled in, I will ask the parents to detail the issue if the child is unable or uncomfortable doing so by themselves. Once the problem has been detailed, I will ask the child what they would like to do about the problem. I like to inject some hope right into the very first session, and I let the child know I want to help him or her in achieving that goal, but that we should probably set up some ground rules so we know what to expect. **Here is a sample script of what to review:**

D: "I know it is a bit strange to meet someone new, but here we are. And I want you to know that meeting you is very important to me, so I will do my best to be here whenever I say I will be, and I hope you will be, too. Don't worry about what we will do, we can always find something to do, and when we meet it is all about you! How exciting is that? I know sometimes people tell you it's not, but right now, it actually is all about you.

My biggest rule in here is just safety. That means, I keep you safe from everyone, even yourself. You noticed my office seems pretty safe, right? I try to keep it cozy and clean for you. But sometimes I might accidentally make you feel upset or even unsafe. If that ever happens, I just want you to put your hands up in the air (demonstrate). Or, you know what? Just one hand can do it. If you do that, I will immediately stop what I am doing and help you feel better.

I'm going to do the same thing for you. When I see you starting to get upset or maybe getting stuck in a bad thought, I am going to put my hands up in the air and say "Whoa!" That will be our signal to each other that we need to calm down and take a break. Do you think that might work?"

If the child doesn't seem receptive to these ideas, ask him or her what they would do instead and adopt those changes if they are appropriate.

Now this is one of the parts of my job I really love—introducing children to my magic rug. In my office I have a small area rug that I purchased at a yard sale. It is pretty raggedy, but kids seem to like it. I use the rug to introduce kinetic activity into anxiety management. Here is an example of how to do so:

D: "Hey, did you see my rug? It's not much to look at, but it actually is very special. I had it imported from Tegucigalpa! What makes this rug special is that it eats emotions. So when you come in here feeling upset, I need you to go onto the rug and shake all of your bad feelings out. My rug will eat them all up and you will feel much better. Do you have some music you like to listen to that helps you to shake it up a little? I can get some for you and maybe that will make it even more fun! We can try it out now if you like. Can I join you? It's been a pretty long day and I could really use some shaking up!"

When you introduce kinetic activity to children, you help them to release all of the tension they store in their bodies all day. It's easy to forget children are not meant to be seated and quiet all day: Their bodies are made to run and jump and shout! When they don't get to do that, the body tends to tense up and they may have outbursts of energy at the most inopportune times.

I let children know it is important to let the body move around. I tell them when we have a bunch of energy inside, it's like having a can of unopened soda that has been all shaken up: you can feel the energy inside, bouncing around. If you pop the top, what happens? The soda explodes out of the can, making a huge mess. But if you let the soda in the can calm down a bit and slowly open up the top, it will not blow up. Instead, it will hiss a bit, but it won't make a big mess. Our bodies are the same way: We have to let all of that energy out of our bodies to allow them to relax a bit.

If the child is quite invested in this kinetic activity, I will encourage their parents to introduce regular ways to manage their energy. Simply allowing them to run around after school for 15 minutes is enough, but other options include letting a child use a bouncing ball you sit on or jumping rope. Work with the family to brainstorm ways the child can get more exercise, and remind parents that their bodies naturally need to use all of that amazing energy they have.

I had one little guy who just wanted to run all over the place, so his mother decided to let him vacuum the house. She had the cleanest house in town and her son instantly started to feel better!

Chapter
5

THE GENERAL,
THE ANXIOUS DRAGON

Remember how I told you about Adalinda the Noble way back at the beginning of this book? She was the one who led us to this fair village and away from the dangers of the world we were in. She was beloved for her kindness and level-headed thinking and she in turn had a great love for her people. It is this love in fact that allows her to still watch over us as, even in spirit. You see, love is always enduring and helps her to reach out to those who need her. It is said that in times of great need, she reveals herself to her devoted dragons and will guide them to good decisions. You can ask her any question and she will help you find the best answer.

The General

What would you do if you could get the answer to any question? Would it make you feel better? Or might the answer itself present some other questions? Our very own General faced this very question not too long ago.

This is a picture of the General.

Pretty awesome, right? He is in charge of our little village. He helps keep us safe and is always interested in the comings and goings of our happy residents.

But the General has a little secret. Ever since the grand undertaking when we established the little village of Longwei, he has been having some trouble focusing. He worries about when we had to leave our old homes, and he thinks about what might happen if something terrible like that ever happens again. He tries not to think about it, but he finds it happening more often than he wants to admit.

"How can I be the leader and be scared?" the General pondered.

The General has been trying to hide it, but Mama Gumbo was onto him. She has a sixth sense about things like that. One night when she was preparing his very favorite dish, she noticed him looking sad. She asked him if something was bothering him.

"No, there's nothing wrong. Things are going great. Everyone is safe and we have your amazing food to enjoy. Look at the weather; it is so sunny and warm. The village is doing just wonderful."

"Sometimes it's not about what's happening outside. It's about what's going on inside here," Mama said, pointing at the General's heart.

The General thought about what Mama Gumbo had said. It was true that things were going well in the village, perhaps better than ever before. Could it be the problem was inside the General's own head? Could it be he was worrying even though nothing really bad was happening? The very idea was strange.

The General went to take a walk by the Lake of Sorrow, as it always helped him to think. He wondered how he could be an effective leader if he was scared all the time. He found himself growing more and more worried every day. What if they really needed him and he couldn't think clearly enough to take decisive action? He would be a failure, a fraud! The General was embarrassed to find himself starting to cry. If he couldn't take care of his village, what good was he? What happens when the person everyone depends on falls apart?

The General stared into the pool and saw a strange light.

He leaned in for a closer look and a small, purple light arose from the water and started to sparkle. It floated up from the water and beckoned for him to follow. The sparkle led him through the woods. Like magic, the sparkle suddenly took the shape of our once great leader, Adalinda.

"General," she said, "Welcome. I have heard your great cry and have come to help you."

"But why?" asked the General. "I have failed you, and our people. I have fear in my heart. I cannot be brave like you."

"Dear General," she said, "It is not fear that ruins a leader. It is fear that makes him strong, makes him the best leader possible. It is fear that helps him to make good choices and to protect his village. Now, what is your question?"

The General thought long and hard. This was a once in a lifetime opportunity. He had to use it wisely. He had to find out why he couldn't be the leader his village needed.

"I have one question, yes. Why am I so full of fear when there is really nothing to be afraid of? And how can I take good care of my village if I cannot be fearless?"

"General, fear is not always something we can see or hear. It is sometimes something we have in our heart. When you find fear in yourself, you must not run from it. You have to look at it long and hard and find out how to manage it. Tell me, what is it you are afraid of? What do you think will happen?"

The General explained he was worried the dragons might again be forced from their home due to something they could not predict.

"General, we cannot predict everything that will happen. We must only know in our hearts that we will be able to handle anything presented to us. I was fearful many times when I was your leader. It was the fear that made me take care of our people and help them find safe places to be. I listened to my little fear voice all of the time. Sometimes it was nothing to worry about, just a little check-in to remind me to be aware not only of things around me but also that I am taking good care of myself. A good leader has to be a role model, and a good leader knows when to lean on friends for help and support. You have to teach others to care for themselves by caring for yourself, and show them how to manage their fears by managing your own."

"But won't they think less of me if I'm not perfect?" the General asked.

Adalinda the Noble laughed, a happy, tinkling sound. "My goodness, no! Nobody's perfect, General. The people respect you when you are honest, and they will help you through your problems. None of us should be alone." With that, she vanished.

The General was surprised to wake up in his own bed. Was it all a dream? It couldn't be! He wondered what he should do. He went back to speak with Mama Gumbo. Adalinda had said he shouldn't go it alone. Maybe talking with a friend would help.

"Mama Gumbo, I think I have a problem," the General began.

"Mmm-hmm," she answered. "So," she said, putting down a bowl of his favorite pudding, "What are we going to do about it?"

The General told Mama Gumbo all about his worries, as well as his visit from Adalinda.

"Are you doing what she said? Taking good care of yourself? When is the last time you took a day off, or went for a long walk? Have you been playing your guitar or spending time with friends?" Mama Gumbo asked.

The General explained his duties in the village kept him very busy. He couldn't even remember the last time he had taken some time for himself. "If I take time for myself, what if something bad happens? I would feel so selfish."

"We will handle it, you silly General. The best leaders inspire their people! You inspire us to help *you* for a change. If you don't take care of yourself you will only feel worse. Please, relax a little! I know some great ways to help you. But first," she said, picking up her phone, "you are taking the day off. Let me make some calls."

The General was surprised that the village was so willing to let him take the day off. They all rose up to help him! To help him to relax, the General turned to his pal, Galen. Galen runs a local yoga and meditation center and was more than happy to help the General learn some relaxing poses.

His friend Jojo encouraged him to join his band, and they all got together to jam. It was so much fun to play his guitar with friends!

Doctor Prudens helped the General learn more about maintaining a healthy diet and taught him about how his body talks to him. The General was amazed to find out that when he is upset he tends to get a stomachache! The doctor suggested that he begin keeping track of his feelings so he can be more aware of his emotional needs and feel less stressed.

Even I helped out! I offered to go on a hike with him the next time he wanted. I hike a lot because I am always finding new places to explore!

And with the help of his family and friends, the General found his worries lessened. He started to feel better, and even though he still got worried sometimes, he was able to use the new skills he had learned to help himself get past it. He realized feeling fear isn't a flaw, it's a strength.

Have you ever felt like the General? He was feeling worried a lot. Do you ever feel worried? To help him when he was feeling worried, Doctor Prudens gave him a form to fill out to help him keep track of his worries. It's on pages 42 & 43. If you fill this out even just once a week, it will help you know how you are feeling. Like the General always says, knowledge is power!

The General's friends and family helped him find ways to calm himself down, and they started with things he already enjoys doing.

FUN WAYS TO MANAGE STRESS!

What are some things you like to do? Make a list of things you enjoy doing:

_____

_____

_____

_____

Now, go back to your list and let's talk about how you feel when you do things you enjoy. Pick your very favorite activity and write down how you feel when you are doing it.

_____

_____

_____

_____

When do you like to do these things? Let's come up with times to schedule them! **Write your activities into the schedule on the next page** and come up with times to schedule them.

MY LIST OF THINGS I ENJOY DOING

Sunday	Monday	Tuesday	Wednesday	Thursday	Friday	Saturday

To help the General manage his bad feelings, Galen suggested he work with his five senses. They're always with you! Galen first started with the General's ears. What do you like to hear? Our ears can transport us to a new, magical place. What do you like to hear to calm you down? To rev you up? It doesn't have to be music, it can be an animal sound, or a noise you like. The General really likes music, so Galen suggested that he make a playlist of songs he enjoys to help him feel better. He also encouraged him to play more music with his friends.

You can listen to any kind of music you like. And not just happy songs; sad songs can also help to get us in touch with our feelings. The General made a playlist of different songs: ones that make him happy, make him think, remind him of times with friends. He also likes to hear the sounds of the wind near Tolkien's Peak. When he feels a bit stressed, he can listen to these sounds to help him feel more grounded. A few deep breaths and some calming music and the General feels much better!

The space you're in really affects how you feel. Did you know being surrounded by things you *don't* like to see can actually upset your mood? The General's room was a mess!

Galen explained that sometimes the outside environment reflects inner trouble. He suggested that the General make sure his environment reflects the mood he wants to be in. Being surrounded by chaos and confusion makes us feel chaotic and confused ourselves. Think about your space: Do you have an area just for you? What types of things do you like in your space? Galen helped the General clean up his space, and what a difference!

What do you like to touch? What do you hate to touch? Galen asked the General what he likes to feel or wear when he wants to feel better. At first, the General had some trouble coming up with any ideas. After all, he tends to wear the same things all of the time. But then he remembered the little bear his mother gave him when he was just a youngling. It always makes him feel good! Galen suggested the General cuddle his bear when he is upset and think about how happy it makes him. Here is a picture of him. Can you draw a picture of you with something that makes you feel happy when you touch it?

While we are on the topic, let's talk about your body. Your body can get very tense when it feels anxious. It can feel all tied in knots! There are many ways to relax your body. A really easy way is to actually make your body a little more stressed in order to force it to relax. It sounds crazy, but it actually works! This is called progressive muscle relaxation. It is very easy. You just go through each part of the body and tighten it so it can calm down.

Remember how we talked about moving around to help get rid of nervous energy? The General thought he would try that as well. You can exercise, or do something physical you like. The General likes walking his nerfle, Georgia, and swimming. What do you like to do?

Galen then told the General something he didn't know: Your sense of smell is the strongest way to help store a memory. Galen explained that if the General could think of a time when he felt really safe and happy, they could try to match this memory with a scent attached to it. Then whenever the General experiences that scent, he will have a positive memory to calm himself. The General thought and thought.

The General recalled that whenever he smells roses, he thinks of his Great Grandma Ruby.

"She always gave the best hugs!" he said.

Galen suggested the General keep a little spray bottle of rose-scented liquid in his desk for times when he feels really worried, and then think of his Great Grandma Ruby giving him a warm hug.

"Her hugs always made me think everything would be all right, and you know what? It always was!" the General exclaimed.

What smells do you like? Are there any smells that remind of you of something positive? We can use those smells to feel help you better. Here are some ideas.

SCENTS SENSE

Did you know that you can use different smells to help you feel better? Here are some of my favorites:

Bergamot: This smells like a lemony-orange and it is very refreshing when you are feeling overwhelmed.

Cedarwood: Like a forest of tall trees in a bottle, this scent helps stabilize your mood when you are feeling overstimulated.

Chamomile: A tiny, daisy-like flower, this little blossom really helps you calm down.

Clary sage: This gentle scent helps with anxiety and improves self-confidence.

Copaiba: A honey-scented resin, this helps those who feel burdened by their problems.

Eucalyptus: This minty leaf gives you a little pick-me-up when you are feeling stressed.

Grapefruit: One sniff of this fruit will help you to feel focused.

Lavender: This pretty purple plant helps you sleep.

Lemongrass: This pleasant scent helps manage agitation and stress.

Lilac: This is traditionally used to help with sleep, but can also help with everyday relaxation.

Lime: This tart fragrance helps you feel more positive about yourself.

Mandarin: This citrusy scent is traditionally used to calm excitability.

Orange: This uplifting scent helps improve the mood when you are feeling down.

Peppermint: Just like a candy cane, this scent helps you think clearly.

Pine: A deep, woodsy scent, it helps you relax your mind.

Rose: This lovely floral scent is calming and uplifting.

Sandalwood: This scent has many uses, including sleep, calming anger, and relaxing the brain.

Tea tree oil: A super helpful oil, this little multi-tasker works on everything from stress to dandruff—who knew?

Vanilla: Described as calming, relaxing, and comforting, this scent is like a warm hug.

There are many ways to use these scents; here are just a few:

1. **Inhale directly:** Rub 1-2 drops into your cupped palms and take a long, deep breath.
2. **Rub directly:** Rub 1-2 drops of oil into your temples, wrists or anywhere, for full body relaxation.
3. **Use on-the-go:** Put a few drops on a handkerchief, cotton pad, or on a scarf and inhale as needed.
4. **Add to your shower:** Immerse yourself in an essential oil steam by adding a couple of drops in your shower.
5. **Use a diffuser:** To get long-lasting benefit, use a diffuser.

Remember: These oils are small but powerful! It's best to start small by testing a small drop on the arm to make sure you are not allergic. If you have special skin concerns, consult your doctor first before trying any of these regimens. Once you know how your body reacts to these scents, relax and enjoy!

MAMA GUMBO'S GOOD MOOD FOOD

Mama Gumbo then helped the General with the last sense: taste. Did you know there are plenty of foods that help your body manage anxiety?

Here's Mama's menu for a Good Mood Meal!

What you feed your body helps feed your mood! There are many foods that help us feel better. Here are just a few. Mama Gumbo keeps them on her menu so all her little dragons stay happy *and* healthy. As always, do not consume any food product you are allergic to, and do not make any specific dietary changes without consulting with your doctor.

Almonds: Find yourself getting a cold more often? Almonds are good at building up your immune system to keep you healthy. As a bonus, they also help if you have headaches when you are stressed. It's a win-win!

Apricots: Apricots are rich in magnesium, which is known as the mineral muscle relaxant of the body. Have you ever tried Epsom salts? The key ingredient is magnesium! So even soaking in magnesium calms your body down. Try dried apricots dried for a fun, portable snack.

Avocado: They may be a little weird-looking on the outside, but on the inside avocados are great at slowing down your heart when it feels like it wants to jump out of your chest.

Bananas: If avocados aren't your thing, unpeel a banana! They have the same effect on your heart and taste better in cereal. Avocados and cereal? YUCK!

Chocolate: Chocolate actually does help us feel better. However, you only need a little and the darker the chocolate, the better you feel. So have a small amount of dark chocolate and feel better fast.

Green, leafy vegetables: When we get stressed, we tend to get sick more easily. Green, leafy vegetables like broccoli or kale help rebuild the immune system and keep you healthy. Remember, healthy bodies are calm bodies!

Oranges: The Vitamin C in oranges helps calm your body down by reducing the hormone that makes your body go into "fight or flight" mode. An apple a day may keep the doctor away, but oranges help, too!

Pistachios: These yummy nuts help you avoid melting down by reducing your heart rate. So, if you feel like your heart is pounding, try a handful of pistachios.

Salmon: Fish have all types of heart-healthy benefits, and salmon in particular helps out with calming the body down and reducing your "fight or flight" response. Maybe that's why fish are so calm?

Spinach: If green, leafy vegetables are your thing, spinach should be your go-to for muscle relaxation. Like apricots, spinach is full of magnesium and will help your body feel calmer.

Sweet potatoes: These tasty spuds are perfect for balancing out sweetness and fullness. They help us focus and keep our tummies full when we are worried.

Turkey: Ever feel sleepy after Thanksgiving dinner? This is because turkey is chock full of an amino acid, L-tryptophan, that helps us relax. Tasty and calming!

Walnuts: These wrinkly nuts have the same effect as pistachios, but some people like them better. Guess it's just a matter of taste!

Mama Gumbo's Lunch Special:

Turkey sandwich with baby spinach
Dried apricots and/or an orange
Sweet potato fries
Dark chocolate tart

Sometimes when we are stressed our tummy starts to ache. Mama Gumbo's got you covered for that, too! Here are her go-to foods to solve tummy troubles:

Bread Products: Any bread product can help a bit to absorb acid in the stomach that can make you feel rumbly or even like you might throw up. Mama Gumbo likes dry toast (meaning toast with nothing on it) or crackers best.

Ginger: Ginger is known to help reduce the feeling of wanting to throw up, which we call nausea. You can try it in many ways, but Mama Gumbo likes ginger chews the best because they taste good and they look like candy. Some of them even stretch and bend like taffy!

Peppermint: This happy flavor helps focus you and ease your stomach. You can find it in candy canes, mints, and even peppermint teas. Mama Gumbo makes a fun, dark-chocolate covered peppermint candy I just love to eat!

Rice: Rice is fantastic at soaking up stomach acid. Mama makes hers with brown rice, but any kind will do.

Diagnosing Anxiety

Generalized anxiety disorder (GAD) is an often undiagnosed phenomena, as it can present as other disorders. Remind yourself that the diagnosis for generalized anxiety disorder is defined in the *Diagnostic and Statistical Manual of Mental Disorders, 5th Edition* as:

1. Excessive anxiety and worry (apprehensive expectation), occurring more days than not for at least six months, about a number of events or activities (such as work or school performance).

2. The individual finds it difficult to control the worry.

3. The anxiety and worry are associated with three (or more) of the following six symptoms (with at least some symptoms having been present for more days than not for the past six months). Note: Only one item required in children.

   - Restlessness, feeling keyed up or on edge.
   - Being easily fatigued.
   - Difficulty concentrating or mind going blank.
   - Irritability.
   - Muscle tension.
   - Sleep disturbance (difficulty falling or staying asleep, or restless, unsatisfying sleep).

4. The anxiety, worry, or physical symptoms cause clinically significant distress or impairment in social, occupational, or other important areas of functioning.

5. The disturbance is not attributable to the physiological effects of a substance (e.g., a drug of abuse, a medication) or another medical condition (e.g., hyperthyroidism).

6. The disturbance is not better explained by another medical disorder (e.g., anxiety or worry about having panic attacks in panic disorder, negative evaluation in social anxiety disorder [social phobia], contamination or other obsessions in obsessive-compulsive disorder, separation from attachment figures in separation anxiety disorder, reminders of traumatic events in

post-traumatic stress disorder, gaining weight in anorexia nervosa, physical complaints in somatic symptom disorder, perceived appearance flaws in body dysmorphic disorder, having a serious illness in illness anxiety disorder, or the content of delusional beliefs in schizophrenia or delusional disorder).

So, what does this all mean? Simply put, it means we are looking for a pattern of behavior that is making a strong negative impact on the person's life. The pattern part is important, as everyone has times they are anxious, and it actually help us out. It becomes a disorder when it begins to happen repeatedly in such a way that it is disruptive to daily life.

Typically the first thing we need to do when diagnosing GAD is to distinguish it from any other disorder. On the following page, you will find the Adverse Symptoms Decision Tree to help you differentiate between the various types of anxiety disorders we will be exploring. I find it much easier to use a decision tree to help me out, so let's get our tree on!

ADVERSE SYMPTOMS DECISION TREE

Physical Symptoms

Restlessness

Tremulous

Easily fatigued

Difficulty concentrating

Mind going blank

Muscle tension

Sleep disturbance

Sweating

Heart palpitations

Nausea/Diarrhea

↓

Is the patient utilizing more medical resources?

↓ Yes

Can you rule out medical issues such as hypothyroidism, temporal lobe epilepsy, endocrine dysfunction, pheochromocytoma, or cardiac illness?

↓ Yes

Is there caffeine or other stimulant abuse?

No →

Psychological Symptoms

Fear

Anxiety

Tension

Worry

Apprehension

Easily startled

Agitation

Irratibility

↓

Can you rule out substance use?

↓ No

Identify harmful substance use, educate patient about the dangers of such abuse; initiate treatment for substance abuse PRIOR to beginning anxiety treatment.

Functional Changes

Avoiding daily responsibilities; relationship disruption; avoiding leaving the house; increase in somatic complaints; increase in self-medicating (food, alcohol, drugs)

↓

Is there functional impairment?

↓ No

Does the patient show a lack of interest in things that are normally enjoyed, or does the patient lack motivation to complete daily tasks? Has the patient experienced significant weight changes? Does the patient endorse suicidal ideation or attempts?

↓ Yes

Assess patient for depression and determine if this is co-occurring or singular (is the patient anxious *and* depressed or just one of the two?). Typically, depression becomes the primary focus of treatment initially due to safety concerns involved with depression and suicidal tendencies.

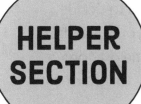

Sample Generalized Anxiety Disorder Treatment Plan

For the clinicians out there, once you have settled on GAD as your diagnosis, you will need to set up a treatment plan. Here is a sample:

Goal: Reduce the overall frequency, intensity, and duration of the anxiety so daily functioning is no longer impaired. Stabilize anxiety level while increasing ability to function on a daily basis. Resolve the core conflict that is the source of anxiety. Enhance ability to effectively cope with the full variety of life's anxieties.

Objective One: Describe current and past experiences with the worry and anxiety symptoms along with their impact on functioning and any attempts to resolve it. Complete any needed psychological tests designed to assess worry and anxiety symptoms. Cooperate with an evaluation by a physician for psychotropic medication, if necessary.

Objective Two: Learn about the cognitive, physiological, and behavioral components of anxiety and its treatment. Learn and implement calming skills to reduce overall anxiety and manage anxiety symptoms. Verbalize an understanding of the role that cognitive biases play in excessive irrational worry and persistent anxiety symptoms.

Objective Three: Identify, challenge, and replace biased, fearful self-talk with positive, realistic, and empowering self-talk. Engage in gradual repeated imaginal exposure to the feared negative consequences predicted by worries and develop alternative reality-based predictions. Learn and implement problem-solving strategies for realistically addressing worries.

You'll notice it is very important to rule out any medical issues first, so having a physician involved right from the beginning is a very good idea. Think of it like this: When you have a cold, you have a fever and maybe a runny nose. Those are two symptoms you can find in *many* disorders, from a simple cold all the way to pneumonia and hypothermia!

You wouldn't want a doctor to rely on just those two symptoms to decide on your course of treatment. You could end up worse than when you started! So in psychology, we do the exact same thing. I always remind my little dragons, a symptom does not make a diagnosis: you need all of the elements to determine the best path of treatment.

One of my best tools in diagnosing GAD is observation, and I suggest you try it as well. Do you *see* psychomotor agitation or sweating? Do you *hear* something that makes you think the child may be experiencing anxiety such as pressured speech or a stutter? Physical symptoms help you determine if an anxiety response is occurring.

My next step is to find out how the child is experiencing anxiety. I let them know it is important for them to be able to tell how it is affecting them, as they are the expert when it comes to how they are doing. Here are some questions to ask:

- Do you think you might worry more than other people?

- Do you sometimes miss out on things you would like to do because you feel worried?

- Do you make up excuses not to do things, even if they are things you like?

- Do you have trouble leaving someone you love, even for something like school or another scheduled occasion?

- Are you unable to complete a task, like homework, because you are worried you won't do it right?

Helping Children Cope with Anxiety

If the child is telling you that the worry is now robbing them of enjoyable time, you are looking at a pretty clear anxiety disorder. I also rely heavily on the observations of people who love them to help determine how the child is doing, especially if the child is somewhat unaware of his or her own behaviors, potentially due to age or development.

It is very important to normalize the experience of anxiety for children. Decide on what to call it. Worries? Anxiety? One of my patients used to refer to it as "bats in the belly" because that was how she experienced the physical sensation of feeling fearful.

I often tell patients that anxiety can be a very good thing! It helps us remember to study for tests, or not to eat food that is too hot. It reminds us to look both ways when we cross the street and not to feed wild animals. There are also many people who use anxiety in their daily lives to help others, such as first responders or detectives. These people use their powerful observation skills to help others.

Unfortunately for children with diagnosable anxiety, the anxiety itself is just a bit too intense right now.

Our job is to turn down the volume. Encourage them to talk with you about times when their anxiety was just right: times it helped them out. You want to really shift their perspective and help them see their anxiety as a blessing, not a curse. To help their parents understand this, there are several books they can peruse. I especially enjoy recommending *The Gift of Fear* by Gavin DeBecker to parents to help them understand this concept. The book talks about the many boons of anxiety as well as how to support someone who has this disorder without judgment.

In the children's section, we went over using the five senses to help patients calm themselves. I like interventions that are very covert in nature. Ultimately, a child well-versed in anxiety techniques can find anything in his or her environment to aid with calming themselves down. This is why we give them lots of options: things to see, things to smell, even things to eat! I have even used a simple tube of peppermint lip balm to calm a child in the past. I let kids know that's what it means to be a ninja therapist. Ninjas are stealthy and use things in their environment to their advantage. No need for special tools when you can use anything at all!

This also presents a very important part of anxiety treatment: personal responsibility. As much as we all want to remove these feelings from a child, ultimately it is their job to help themselves. It is empowering for kids to know they can rely on themselves for positive mood stability, and it allows them to have appropriate expectations of what the environment will do for them when they are upset. I remind kids that, "You are responsible for making you feel better, not anyone else. My job is to teach you how. Once you learn the techniques that work best for you, they are yours forever. Who knows, maybe you will help someone else one day!"

It is important to note that children in the grips of anxiety tend to feel disconnected from their bodies. When your nervous system is constantly being activated, you get used to the feeling of tension and don't notice if it increases. This is oftentimes why anxious children have "mystery bruises" from all types of injuries they don't even notice because the body is under attack all the time. What's one more bump?

Any form of exercise and especially yoga can help anxious children (and pretty much anyone) to reconnect with their bodies so they know when they are feeling poorly. They have to be connected to their bodies in order to know when to use their tools: otherwise, they will not be able to master their anxiety response. The primary reason anxiety tools fail is because the child doesn't know when to use them. It's a much better idea to calm your body down before you reach the point of no return rather than after you've been crying and screaming for hours.

Speaking of which, there are a number of ways to increase a child's mindfulness of their body's reaction to stress. The first step is to help the child to tap into how he or she is feeling on a daily basis. Use the Anxiety Log on pages 42 & 43.

This is a really easy one, and I sometimes will do it in session with younger children while I ask older children initially to complete one of these daily. If you have a child who is more invested in using a technological solution, they can use one of any number of cell phone/tablet applications. Some of my favorites include Mood Panda and My W Days. Be aware that both of these applications have a social media aspect, which you can turn off in the application settings. I suggest that, if parents are going to have their children use these apps, they turn off this feature to prevent cyber bullying and the potentially exploitive behaviors that occur regularly in the internet world.

Establishing Healthy Sleep Patterns

Does anyone know where bedtime went? I can't even tell you how often I ask a parent when the child typically goes to bed and I am met with confused stares. All children, not just anxious children, like routine as it makes them feel safe. It is important that children have regular wake and sleep times. Sometimes the first thing you have to do is simply establish a regular bedtime routine.

I will first ask the parent to ascertain what time the child typically falls asleep. I let parents know this may require a few days or even weeks of observation to establish a clear understanding of when the child's body is naturally falling asleep. I also need to know if the child is napping during the day, as this will impact the sleep cycle. As much as possible, I want the parent to discourage napping unless the child is under the age of five, wherein naptime may be part of a regular daycare routine.

Once we have established when the child sleeps, we need to figure out if the child is getting enough sleep. Does the child appear fatigued, or groggy? You should rule out any medical issues right at the start of treatment, so you will know if there is a medical reason that sleep would be impaired.

Once you know when the child falls asleep, you will want to work with the child's family to determine a more appropriate sleep time. This is when the real work on sleep training begins. This is a tough thing to do, and requires cooperation from both caregivers and the child. It can also take a significant period of time to really get it in place. **On the next page is a guide to sleep training.**

GUIDE TO SLEEP TRAINING

1. Observe the sleep pattern for at least seven days. Make note of wake time, sleep time, and any nap times. Also note periods of extremely high or extremely low energy.

2. A caregiver or clinician will examine these patterns and determine the first sleep pattern (e.g., when the child is falling asleep naturally). Once this is established, the child and family agree to have the child wake and sleep at the same time every day, *including weekends.* The child will then go to bed nightly 30 minutes before this established sleep time to help him or her wind down with lights out at the designated sleep time.

3. The family and child will also agree on a sleep time goal. Initially, the child will simply fall asleep at the designated time for about a week or so until he or she is naturally tired at that time. Bed time will then be pushed back in 30 minute increments establishing natural tiredness until the desired sleep time is attained.

4. The child will agree on a wind-down routine — a routine the child will follow nightly to prepare the body for sleep. The most salient parts of such a routine include the following:
   • Decide on when the child will begin readying for sleep.
   • Establish grooming activities, such as brushing teeth, washing the face, or getting into his or her pajamas.

5. Decrease exposure to exciting media an hour before bed. By excitable, I mean whatever makes the child feel excited. This clearly means no adrenaline scares or horror movies, but also avoid media that the child becomes very invested in. For example, if the child is a big Batman fan and gets very energetic when watching anything with Batman in it, those items are off limits one hour before bed.

6. Do not allow the child access to items with a blue backlight an hour prior to sleep. This includes cell phones, laptops, and tablets. We do this because that light tends to activate the math area of the brain, which switches the body's thinking processes back on and prevents the mind from relaxing. I remind

parents that children have no actual reason to have access to their technology prior to sleep unless there is no responsible adult available to them to help them handle any issue that may arise. If this is the case, clearly a larger situation is occurring and requires attention.

7. Anywhere from an hour prior to sleep to directly before bed, you want to raise the internal body temperature. You can do this any number of ways: the child can bathe in hot water or consume a warm, decaffeinated beverage. This is a good opportunity to use herbs that aid with relaxation. Things such as lavender, chamomile, and valerian are excellent in aiding relaxation and can be ingested as well as used topically. Remember, always check with a physician about adding these items into the child's diet.

8. Finally, many children will report they have difficulty sleeping. A progressive muscle relaxation can help, as well as reading a relaxing novel. I often suggest children read about a subject they find particularly boring to help them sleep.

Managing Anxiety Before Bed

One of the things that can impact sleep adversely is the emergence of anxious thoughts just as you are trying to rest. Why does this happen? It is an interesting phenomena. Think of it like this: you wake up tired, so all of your active energy is focused on getting through the day. Walking, talking, and responding to others. When you are tired, this can feel like a Herculean effort! All of your anxieties end up taking a backseat to just getting through the day. So when you finally get to your bed and the lights are out, the lack of stimuli causes all of those set aside anxieties to overflow into your consciousness. Before you know it, your brain is wide awake and asking all sorts of questions.

The best way to handle this is to shut these thoughts down quickly in a modified form of thought-stopping. The first thing you need to know about the technique we will employ here is an understanding of how the brain works. Your brain cannot contemplate self-negatives. This means that when you tell your brain not to think about something (as we so often do with a perseverative thought), that very thought is reinforced and then will gain even more momentum in repeating itself. So when you have a thought that comes up and you tell yourself, "Don't think about that," what your brain hears is "*DO* think about that!"

We are going to use our brain's own natural tendency to reinforce self-negatives against itself. So what you will do is when your child patient tells you they are having a perseverative thought, encourage him or her to say the thought out loud. You then will remind the child that thoughts are just thoughts, *not actions*. They do not cause anything to happen and they do not stop anything from happening. Let them know that it is fine to think their thought as much or as often as they wish; however, you must caution them to never, *never ever,* under any circumstances, think about PINK ELEPHANTS. Do *not* think about pink elephants. Don't do it! No thinking about pink elephants!

When they do this, you want them to really have fun with it. Notice when they think about the elephants: they will usually smile or even giggle. "You're doing it right now, you're thinking about the pink elephants, aren't you? Now what did I just tell you? NO pink elephants!"

Let them know that by thinking about the elephants, they stopped their thoughts, even for a few small seconds. If they can stop their thoughts for even a few seconds, they can begin to gain back non-worry time in their lives. Soon they can have a minute back, then five, and one day they will be able to decide *when* and for *how long* they will worry. They can control their thoughts! THIS is a monumental occasion—for the first time, this child took absolute control of that anxious brain. Make sure you really celebrate the moment so the child knows how important this is.

Really encourage them to practice the pink elephants as much as possible in order to begin gaining control over their thoughts, and reinforce them whenever they do so. Let them know this is a tough thing to do and that they are very brave to keep at it.

To manage those annoying bedtime thoughts, creating a worry space prior to bed can be highly effective. For children who are literate, I suggest having them pick up a blank notebook to use specifically as an anxiety log. I encourage kids to decorate it however they please and fill it however they wish, but they need to use it daily. Two hours prior to bedtime or an hour before dark fall if the anxiety worsens at night. The child will open up the journal and write in every little thing on his or her mind. I remind the child there is no judgment here: Whatever he or she writes won't make anything happen and it doesn't stop anything from happening, it just is. Once they have listed everything going on in their minds, they are to close the book. Thereafter, if any of the thoughts come back they are to say to themselves, *It's fine. It's in the book. I will handle it in the morning.* Let the child know there is nothing at all they have written down that needs to be handled immediately. If a new thought occurs, that thought can be added to the book but the book is then closed.

If the child is too young or not literate, worry dolls are a great alternative. These are small little totems you make to help create an external locus of control to manage the anxiety. That's a fun psychological term meaning we let something outside of us handle the problem, and it makes us feel better. Traditional worry dolls are actually quite small and thus are easily lost; not a great trait in a tool meant to help kids not to worry! To solve this problem, I prefer to make mine out of the old-timey clothespins you get at the craft store, but you can even use Popsicle sticks if you like.

I introduce the worry dolls to children in session and let them know we can make something that will help with their anxiety. I work with the child to decorate a clothespin with any number of things. Paints, markers, pipe cleaners, and googly eyes are some of my favorites. Once we have created our doll, I let the child know that in ancient Mayan culture, they used to make little dolls just like this to help with their worries. At night before you go to bed, you tell your doll all of your worries, no matter how big or small. Whisper them into the worry doll and they will work while you sleep to handle your worries. When you wake up in the morning you can take the worry back if you wish. In session, review with parents how to use the worry dolls and create a sleepy time routine for the dolls, making a bed for them and tucking them in. Check in regularly about the dolls and see if parents are encouraging the child to use them. If so, is it helping?

You are now in a spot where the child should be working on mindfulness daily. Did you know that mindfulness is the number one way to rebuild GABA in the brain? GABA is a neurotransmitter that acts as the brain's brake pedal. It slows thoughts down and it helps the brain to think more clearly. Rebuilding GABA should be one of our top priorities in anxiety work, as it will help the brain to heal itself and safeguard the patient against future anxiety episodes. Mindful breathing, thinking, and feeling all help!

Finally, please be aware that generalized anxiety disorder can co-occur or precede other disorders. Good thing we are about to explore those disorders, right?

As promised, here is a decision tree to help you to determine what other disorders may be present.

ANXIETY DISORDERS DECISION TREE

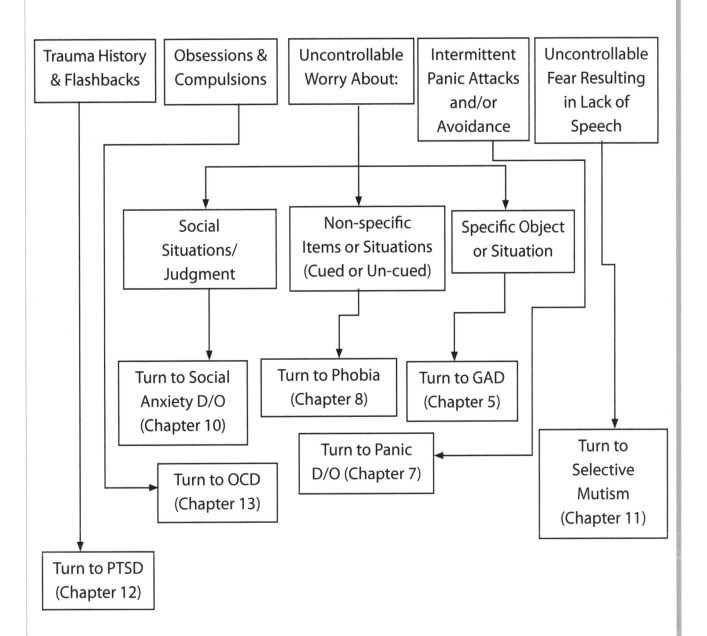

Now you are all set! Feel free to go to the chapter you need or read straight through to get some great therapeutic techniques for any anxiety.

DUPLOS, THE EMOTIONALLY DYSREGULATED DRAGON

Have you ever heard the phrase, "Two heads are better than one?" Well, I think Duplos the two-headed dragon might disagree with you.

Duplos has two heads! Now, that would be fine if they got along all the time, but they really don't. One head is called Dup and the other is called Los, and boy, can they argue! Duplos comes from a long line of two-headed and even ten-headed dragons. They are known to be the wisest among all dragons because they have more brain power (two heads, duh!).

But in Duplos's case, two heads are more a burden than a help. You see, Dup is a braniac: always reading, always reciting facts about various things. He makes all of his decisions based on facts. Los on the other hand leads with his heart: What he feels is real for him. So he would rather feel good about his choices than have them make logical sense, and Dup just can't understand that!

Duplos

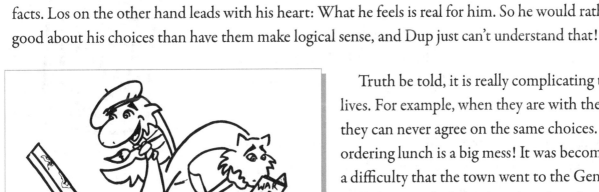

Truth be told, it is really complicating their lives. For example, when they are with their friends they can never agree on the same choices. Even ordering lunch is a big mess! It was becoming such a difficulty that the town went to the General for help. He asked Duplos what they thought he should do to help them.

"Separate us," said Dup simply. "We clearly can't be both intellectual and emotional, so use some magic and make us into two separate dragons."

Los agreed. "I can't bear one more second with that brainy hothead!" he moaned. "Please don't make me deal with him another day!"

The General consulted Mama Gumbo, who was the magical expert in town. She looked through her many books and ingredients to see if such a magic did exist. After much searching, she came up a small potion bottle labeled, "Twine."

Mama Gumbo explained that when she was just a youngling, her great grandmother had created the magic with her in order to separate some crops that had become entangled with each other.

"But the magic had grave consequences," she explained. "The two needed each other to be healthy. All of the crops died once they were separated. Some things must learn to coexist for both to prosper."

"But these are not crops," the General reasoned. "These are younglings! Full of prosperity, and thoughts and dreams! Surely they can survive without each other. They are very different; perhaps they will be healthier separated."

"I disagree," said Mama Gumbo. "Yes, they are different, but they are together for a reason. Though one is logical and one is emotional, a balance must be struck. Logic without emotion can be very dangerous," she warned. "Like the plants that died, so might Duplos wither and sicken if separated. The two must instead learn how to embrace their differences."

Because of the danger this represented, the General agreed not to use the magic and instead put it back in Mama Gumbo's cabinet. But little did they know that sneaky Ember was there, listening in... "Dangerous?" Ember thought. "That sounds like fun!"

The next day on the way to school, Ember just happened to be walking on the same path as Duplos.

"Heard the General won't let you two separate. Tough break." Ember said sweetly—too sweetly!

"Yeah," sniffed Los. "I was so ready to have my own space and now... and now!" He began crying.

"Can you even believe this guy?" asked Dup. "How can I get any studying done when he is constantly crying? Or yelling, or pouting, or whatever? Completely useless, if you ask me. If we cannot be split, then that is a statement of fact and there is no purpose in fighting it."

"Oh, I wouldn't say you *can't* be split," said Ember, brandishing the very magical potion he had smuggled from Mama Gumbo's cabinet.

"How did you—" Dup began.

"I'm resourceful," Ember said slyly, moving the potion just outside of Dup's reach. "Now then. What's it worth to you? To *both* of you?"

Sixty-three crystal gems and three packs of gum later, Duplos had the potion. Ember had explained that they need only to read what was written on it and they would be separated. Both agreed this was a good decision and so they each drank half the potion, said the magic words and BOOM! With a puff of smoke and a clap of thunder, Duplos became Dup and Los!

They rushed home to share their good fortune with their family... but they were not exactly as happy as Dup and Los expected.

"What have you done?" their mother asked. "You are supposed to be together, not apart. How did this happen?"

The two started in on a story they had rehearsed about walking next to Dragon Springs and suddenly having their wish granted by a passing fairy dragon. Although their mother found the story hard to believe, her children were now separated so she figured she would have to get used to it. She immediately called up the General.

"Something's fishy here," the General said as he got off the phone.

"Let it play out," said Mama Gumbo. "The best lessons are those we teach ourselves."

The next day the boys presented to school as two separate dragons. This was a bit confusing, as they only had one desk, and only had one set of books. The teachers explained that each dragon would now be responsible for his own work. They also explained that each dragon could pick whatever extracurricular activities he wanted, as they didn't have to compromise anymore.

Dup was ecstatic that he could finally join the academic clubs he wanted: math club, history club, even the philosophy club. Los was thrilled to be able to join the poetry and drama clubs, and he was looking forward to working on some artwork for the upcoming school art show.

Duplos' friends, however, were a bit confused by this sudden change. They had gotten quite used to having both dragons involved in their games and having only one made them feel like something was missing. It got so bad that their friends began avoiding them. Dup was shocked when he showed up at philosophy club and no one else was in attendance. Los overhead some friends saying he was "just too much" and he was "always upset about something."

The friends realized that avoiding the problem wasn't helping, so they instead asked both brothers to come meet them to talk it over. They explained that Dup was *too* logical and he often did not consider other people's feelings.

"Like how you told me I looked ugly in my new dress!" said his friend Barta.

"But you did," contended Dup. "That color was not at all complimentary."

"But it hurt her feelings!" said Alonko, who used to go swimming with Duplos at Dragon Springs. Since the separation, he never seemed to have time to meet with either Dup or Los to explore the water looking for rare shells and shiny rocks.

Dup crossed his arms in frustration. "Why? I was just telling the truth! Isn't that what friends are supposed to do?'

"Not when it hurts dragon's feelings," Barta sniffled.

"That," Dup huffed, "is entirely illogical." He turned his back to her.

The friends further explained that Los was becoming very hard to work with as he could never make a decision and was highly unreliable.

"You said you'd help me set up for the bake sale," Vlad said.

"Yeah, but I didn't really *feel* like it," Los explained. "I wanted to take a nap instead. So I did!"

"But I was counting on you! We needed your help to raise money for the next drama show, and now we won't have enough funds to get some of the costumes we need." The other friends nodded in agreement.

"Oh, no! Are you mad at me? I simply cannot stand *that*!" And with that, Duplos ran off.

Since neither dragon wanted to listen, their friends decided to continue to avoid spending time with them. When the art show came around, Los' friends did not respond to his carefully made invitations. This made Los understandably upset. He ran into his room and flung himself on his bed in distress.

"I am trying to read," Dup said. "What on earth are you so upset about? Are you injured?"

"Just my heart," wept Los. "I sent out all of these invitations and not one of our friends responded!"

"So?" Dup countered. "You don't need them to win the art show."

Los started to cry even more. "What's the point of winning without good friends to celebrate with you? And what kind of artist has no friends? I must be a terrible artist!"

"That's illogical," said Dup. "Your talent is not

related to your ability to have friends. Being able to draw has nothing to do with being able to spend time with people."

"That's not the point!" exclaimed Los. "There's no point in winning if my friends aren't there with me."

"Also illogical," Dup continued. "You will win regardless of them. Unless of course, they are doing the work for you. You will win on your own merit."

"You never understand! There is more to life than winning and losing!" Los began to sob and sob.

"You're right," Dup said softly. "I don't understand. But I don't like to see you crying, either."

"Because it makes you sad?" Los asked.

"No, because it is loud and irritating. Please cry quietly or not at all. I have to study." Dup went back to his book.

"You know what?" Los started to yell. "I don't even need a brother! Don't talk to me anymore!"

"Sounds fine to me," Dup said.

So the two brothers, already separated from their friends, were now separated from each other as well. Initially they both pretended it didn't bother them, but eventually they both started to feel a bit sad about it... and lonely.

The day of the art show finally arrived.

Although Los felt he had put forth some of his very best work it felt empty without his family or friends to support him. He waited all night in the hopes that he would take home a big fat blue ribbon and prove to everyone what a great artist he was.

But the prizes were given out and Los did not receive even one. All alone, he started to cry.

"I am such a loser!" he yelled at himself. "I'm a terrible artist, and a terrible friend!"
He grabbed his artwork and prepared to throw it in the garbage.

"Hey! I don't think that's true," said a familiar voice.

"Dup? What are you doing here?" Los asked.

"I thought looking at some art work might clear my head. Then I heard you crying. You're wrong, by the way. You are not a terrible artist," Dup said.

"Then why didn't I win?" sniffled Los.

"Any number of reasons," said Dup. "For example, it could be that the judges didn't like the medium you used, or the subject, or for no other reason than they simply did not like it. It could be that you didn't fill out your registration form properly. But honestly, I think it's because you showed up at the bake sale instead of the art show."

The two laughed and hugged.

"Oh, Dup, what would I do without you? I miss you so much!"

"I miss you, too," Dup said. "I find that even though what I say is logical, it sometimes hurts people's feelings. My friends don't want to spend time with me anymore."

"We are better together," they said together.

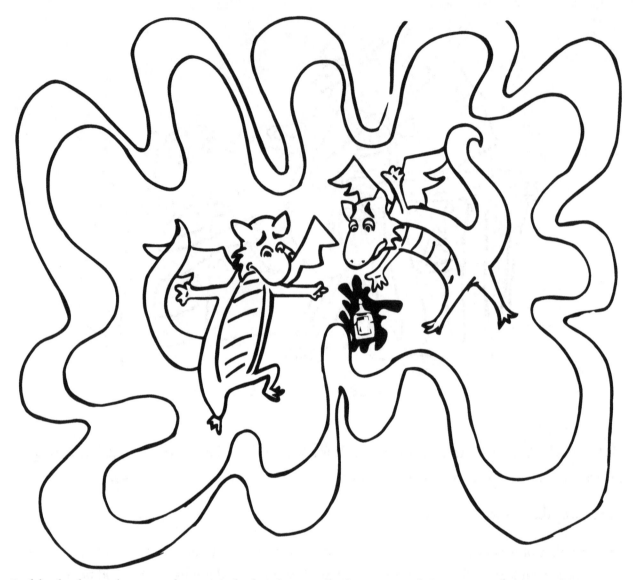

Suddenly the air became electric and a bright purple glow encased the two. They were lifted into the air and the magic potion they had used reappeared.

Dup read, "It says, let what was done, be undone."

"Agreed!" said Los.

They heard a crackle like thunder and there was a buzzing glow, so bright you could see it for miles. All of the town ran toward it, wondering what could cause such a thing. After some time, the light finally died down and what it revealed left the town cheering.

Duplos was whole again! Their parents ran up to give them enormous hugs. Their friends all commented how good it was to have them back together again.

Dup explained, "We realized that brains without a heart just doesn't work!"

Los added, "We may be different, but together we are wise!"

"Together is better," they said.

Have you ever felt like your brain and heart just weren't connecting? That's a common feeling when we are worried or scared. But as the story of Duplos shows, you can't have one without the other. There is actually a type of thinking in which you take your emotional thoughts, combine them with your logical thoughts, and then come up with a wise thought. So basically, I *feel* this, and I *know* that, so I will *do* this. Let Duplos show you!

"Oh no! A spider!" exclaimed Los.

"Well, I know that *particular* spider is not dangerous," Dup said. "In fact, she's pretty friendly. She could stay in our room and not hurt anybody."

Los persisted, "But spiders scare me and I worry she will hurt me anyway! She can't stay in our room! We should squish her!"

"Be reasonable," said Dup. "We can't squish her. She isn't even bothering anyone."

So, the spider *isn't* dangerous, but she still frightens Los… What should Duplos do?

Here's an idea: what if Dup just helped the spider outside? That way, Los isn't scared, the spider is not hurt, and everyone is safe.

That is an example of good problem-solving! Let's do some more! Here are some examples of problems. I want you to think of what Dup and Los might think, and then what a good compromise would be.

Problem One: They have a party they agreed to attend, but Los wants to play video games instead and Dup thinks it will be boring.

Problem Two: Duplos got a bad grade but are afraid to tell their parents.

Why not come up with some problems of your own to solve? Remember, practice makes perfect and the more practice you get, the better problem-solver you will be!

Using DBT for Anxiety

DBT is a great training tool to help anyone make better decisions and handle stress better. Essentially, it is all about bringing an awareness to our own thought processes (mindfulness), then looking into how we handle things that upset us (distress tolerance), and finally, how we keep our emotions in check (emotional regulation).

Mindfulness is an incredibly important tool, but it is often forgotten in our impulsive world. We want things and we want them now! We in the Western world really don't place much value on mindfulness. In fact, we praise people for just the opposite, being able to multi-task. Think carefully about your daily life: How often do you do *just one thing?* You might be reading this right now but also paying attention to your phone, the television, or another person. You may be thinking about what you will have for dinner tonight, or when your rent is due. See how easily we slip out of mindfulness?

Imagine instead a world where we actually give complete attention to just one task at a time. Sounds crazy, doesn't it? But it is essential in anxiety to allow yourself to focus on one thing at a time so that you can stop yourself from being overwhelmed by too many different ideas and allow yourself to manage one small thing at a time.

Building mindfulness is honestly much simpler than you think. Anything can be mindful as long as you give it your full attention. To help children learn about mindfulness, I start by introducing the concept simply. I use an activity called, "Make me a jelly sandwich." This is how you do it.

D: "Guess what? I am super hungry, so do you think you can help me? I want to make a jelly sandwich, but I am not sure how."

(You can use either pretend food or real food. You will need two slices of bread, a jar of jelly, and a butter knife.)

D: "Here is everything we need. Can you explain to me how to make a jelly sandwich? I will follow your directions exactly, and then we can both enjoy a tasty treat!"

This is when the fun begins. You will do everything *exactly* as the child says. For example, if the child were to say, "Put the jelly on the bread," you would take the jar of jelly and place it on the bread. What you want the child to do is to think out every single step. You want them to tell you to take the lid off the jelly before spreading it, and so forth.

Once you are done, you will note how easy it is to rush through something and just assume certain steps. You will let the child know that *this* is the key to mindfulness: taking things slowly, step by step, and enjoying each moment. We have to live in the now rather than anticipating our next step.

As soon as this concept is gained, you want to relate it to a task the child does regularly. For example, if you have a child who practices piano, you can ask them to take five minutes daily and actually play mindfully. Look at the keys, feel them vibrate. Play slowly and enjoy each single note. Explain that this is how mindfulness works. It allows us to slow our thoughts and increase our level of comfort in adversity.

Please understand this is a very simple, beginner mindfulness activity. If you are working with a child who is more advanced, you can move up to an actual guided meditation or even a brush meditation (one of my personal favorites)! But for now, this is all we need.

The Mindfulness Snow Globe

For this activity, you will need the following materials:

1. A mason jar
2. Water
3. Glitter (because you always need glitter)
4. An emollient, such as glycerin, which you can obtain at a craft store, or hair gel
5. Three small plastic objects of differing sizes and shapes

When the child comes in, you will ask him or her if they want to make a snow globe. You will then assemble all of the parts but do not show them the three objects. Typically, I like to pick three small objects that are similar, such as three animals you find in the sea. Drop the three objects in without allowing the child to see them.

Now shake up that snow globe! Place it down in front of the child for a few seconds (three seconds maximum) and take it away, placing it behind your back. Ask the child what he or she saw and let them guess.

Now do it again, but this time allow the globe to stay there for five seconds before taking it away. Again ask the child what he or she saw in the globe. You will do this once more, only allowing for one or two additional seconds of observation.

Finally, give the snow globe the best shake ever and place it down in front of the child. Ask the child to take some deep breaths and to let the breath calm the body down. Have the child observe the glitter as it slowly floats to the bottom. Once everything is completely calm, ask the child what he or she sees inside the globe. Ask the child if it was easier to determine what was inside the globe at the beginning of the activity or at the end. Reinforce that it is hard to understand what is going on when things are chaotic, like they were inside the snow globe.

Now ask the child to pretend that his or her brain is a snow globe. How did the brain feel when the child arrived? Was it very busy and chaotic, like the first snow globe, or was it calm and relaxed, like the last snow globe? Remind the child that we need to calm our thoughts in order to feel better and to understand what is going on around us better. Have the child take the snow globe and use it whenever they feel overwhelmed by simply shaking it and then breathing deeply while the glitter settles.

Let's move on to our second DBT skill: distress tolerance. This is a skill we all need but very few of us enjoy. Distress tolerance includes three main areas: mindfulness of breath, mindfulness of the situation, and mindfulness of ourselves.

Did you know that, when anxious, many people unconsciously hold their breath? That's not good, because the lack of oxygen tends to lead to increasing panic. We need to breathe to live! So the first thing you need to work on is increasing awareness of the breath.

I ask children to work on belly breathing, meaning when the breath comes in, the belly inflates and when the breath leaves, the belly deflates. We practice in session and I ask that they try to work on their breathing initially for one minute a day. Focus on the breath and just allow it to come in and out.

As the child gains mastery, we will increase the time spent on this activity. Once a child has reached five minutes, I typically allow them to self-regulate how much breathing time they need.

It's important the child practices relaxation breathing when they are *not* upset, so that the skills will be automatic when they actually are upset. I ask them to take nice, deep gulps of air when they are happy so they can really enjoy that moment. Let the happiness fill you and stop time for a moment.

Once we are aware of our own breath, we will begin working on mindfulness of situations. That means working on seeing a situation from other perspectives. This is one of the reasons we explored the story of Duplos at the beginning of this chapter. They show you two different perspectives of every problem. A fun way to introduce perspective is to look at the problems at the end of the children's section and engage the child in a discussion of what Dup might do in the situation as compared to Los. You can suggest they draw their answers, sing their answers, or even dance their answers, depending on what type of learning style resonates the best with them.

When the child has gained mastery in imaginary situations, you will begin to transfer this to real situations. When you discuss events of the day, work on looking at different perspectives. Ask, could there be information you don't know that might help you to understand someone's actions or reactions? How do we ask these questions? Rehearse these communication skills and you will really help an anxious child feel safer in various situations, even those they cannot predict. How awesome is that?

The final skill we will focus on is emotion regulation. I remind children that emotions are a gift; we are able to feel things other creatures can't. There is a great strength in allowing an emotion to be fully experienced. But there are also times when our emotions can overwhelm and control us. The first step to managing emotions is helping children identify their emotions. You can use an emotion chart or one of the Anxiety Log on page 42. You can also play a game I like called, "Name That Emotion."

"Name That Emotion" is actually quite simple. You start by identifying an emotion, either by name or by image (I like using emojis or media pictures). Then you talk about when we feel that emotion, if we like that emotion, and how we might be able to access that emotion again. We then talk about what it might feel like to be "trapped" in an emotion, such as anger, and how much energy that takes away from us.

I remind children that difficult emotions are a fine place to visit, but you do not want to live there. We then talk about the costs and benefits of staying in a negative emotional space and work on tactics to help us to move forward.

A final word here: DBT skills are useful throughout life. A child who can master these three small parts of DBT now will be able to manage emotions better as they age and avoid negative anxiety states as they grow. And who doesn't want that?

Chapter

7

JUMPY, THE DRAGON OF PANIC

Jumpy

Jumpy is just a normal little dragon, like you or me, but he has a little problem. Jumpy is feeling a little... well, *jumpy* lately. It all started a week ago when his friend, Rerun, surprised him unexpectedly with a Jack-in-the-box and he's been on edge ever since. He wound and wound and wound the crank and never expected that clown to jump at him! Ever since then, he's been very, very nervous. His heart has been pumping *so* fast, his paws are sweaty, and he feels warm all the time. His friends say he's been very snappy with others and sometimes he gets scared for no reason at all. Jumpy just wants to feel normal again!

Have you ever felt like Jumpy? Lately, Jumpy has felt nervous and panicked a lot of the time. That darn Jack-in-the-box! Even though he tries not to, he finds himself thinking about what happened with the Jack-in-the-box an awful lot. He is even having nightmares about it. Sometimes, he gets so upset thinking about it that it makes him want to cry and his tummy hurts. Jumpy is experiencing something called "panic disorder." This is a condition in which you feel fear and worry along with panic attacks, which is when your body suddenly acts as if it is in danger, sometimes for no clear reason at all. This is what happens when Jumpy thinks about that Jack-in-the-box. Just like you, he feels scared in his body *and* his mind. Even though Jumpy may not actually be in danger, his body acts as if he *is* in danger and this makes him feel even more scared.

Fun Fact 1: Panic disorder is something anyone can feel!

When Jumpy gets upset his body tells him so. Here is a picture of Jumpy and what his body does when he is upset.

ANXIETY IN MY BODY

What does your body do when you are upset? If we listen to our bodies, they will tell us when we are upset even if our brains don't really tell us so. It works in the same way your stomach might growl even though your brain didn't tell you yet that you were hungry. Our bodies are very smart! Can you list what parts of your body react when you are upset?

- _____

- _____

- _____

- _____

- _____

Jumpy's biggest fear when he starts to panic is that he will suddenly stop breathing. How scary is that? Have you ever felt that way?

_____

_____

_____

_____

_____

Well, I'm here to remind you that breathing is automatic, meaning we breathe all the time and don't even need to think about it. However, when we start to think about *not* breathing we can get very scared and it makes it even harder for us to breathe. Not good! So the first thing Jumpy wants you to know is that YOU CAN ALWAYS BREATHE. Seriously, you can. When you start to worry about not breathing, please remind yourself simply, "I can always breathe. Breathe!" It's important that you keep a good flow of air in your lungs to help keep you

calm. For that very reason, your therapist is going to teach you some handy-dandy ways to help you make sure you take some good deep breaths to keep yourself relaxed.

Here are some quick tools to keep you breathing:

1. Take three deep breaths: They act like "control, alt, delete" for your brain!
2. Blow some bubbles: It relaxes you and helps you practice breathing in fully and breathing out in a slow, controlled way.
3. If you are trying to increase your air flow, try using your breath to move a pinwheel, a feather, or even a cotton ball. Make a game of it!

Now we know HOW our bodies panic, but we still don't know why. Well, it's actually a pretty amazing thing! Our brains are wired to keep us safe all of the time. That means if our brains believe there is something dangerous near us (or even thinks about something dangerous) our brains instantly decide they need to keep us safe. Because of the way our brains are made, they actually feel fear before they decide whether to respond to the fear or whether the fear is real or not.

Fun Fact 2: Fear is AUTOMATIC! We get scared before we can even think about whether we should be scared or not.

Simply put, when we see something scary, whether it is a car accident or an imaginary ghost, the brain reacts the same way immediately—with a strong fear reaction. This is why you might walk through a corny haunted house and know a jump-scare is coming, yet you will still have a fear response. Have you ever seen a scary movie and still be scared the second time around? This is why. It's actually pretty hard to talk your brain out of being scared until it is certain you are safe, so don't feel discouraged if it takes a little while to begin getting past your fears.

Now that we know what our bodies do when we are upset, how do we know when our bodies are feeling better? It's important we know when we are feeling better so we know when we are being successful. If we don't, it's sort of like we are running a race but we don't know where the finish line is— how could we ever win that way? Let's talk a little bit about how you want to feel when you know you are doing better. Use the following worksheets to help yourself and Jumpy feel better.

Jumpy understands he's not going to feel better immediately. He has to practice so he can start to feel better, just like you. First, Jumpy will keep track of how upset he gets during the day and how often. It's good to keep track of our feelings so we can help ourselves feel better. Here's the sheet Jumpy will be using to keep track of how he is feeling.

Fun Fact 3: Not everyone panics in the same way, and you can be exposed to the same information at different times and it may not always result in panic symptoms.

THIS is why it's really important to keep track of how you are feeling. You might surprise yourself when sometimes you react better to something that made you upset in the past. What types of things make it more likely that you will feel panicky? For example, maybe if you are hungry or sleepy? Most of us are more edgy when we are cranky, for an example. It can really be helpful if you know what sets you off, so you can plan ahead.

Your therapist is specially trained to help you to feel better. It is important that you let him or her know how you are feeling so they can help you best. Now comes the fun part! He or she has a whole bunch of things to try to help you feel better. Good luck!

I FEEL BETTER WHEN...

When I know I am doing better, I will know because I will feel like this:

_____

I really want to feel like this (because then I'll know I'm feeling better!):

_____

Jumpy knows when he is feeling better! Here are some things he feels when he isn't feeling worried. Circle the feelings you have when you aren't anxious.

Happy	Smiling	Laughing	Warm
Safe	Relaxed	Calm	Light
Loose	Chilled out	Taking it easy	Putting my feet up
Peaceful	Confident	Hopeful	Delighted

JUMPY'S GOALS
FOR FEELING BETTER!

It's always a good idea to set a plan to help yourself feel better!

Here are Jumpy's goals for feeling better:

Goal 1: Be able to take three deep breaths.

Goal 2: Tell my body that I am safe and sound.

Goal 3: If I can't get my fear out of my head, I will change my scene! I can look at a relaxing picture, or one of my toys.

Goal 4: I will not be mean to myself because I get scared! I need to be kind to myself in order to feel better.

Goal 5: Improve how I react, I need to celebrate every time I panic a little less. I can beat this!

Goal 6: To be super brave! I just want to be the best me I can be!

Do you have any goals you would like to write down?

_____

_____

_____

_____

_____

Panic Disorder

Panic disorder is defined in the *DSM-5*® as:

1. Experiencing recurrent, unexpected panic attacks with at least one of the attacks being followed by one month (or more) of one or both of the following:

- Persistent concern or worry about additional panic attacks or their consequences (e.g., losing control, having a heart attack, going crazy).

- Significant maladaptive change in behavior related to the attacks (e.g., behaviors designed to avoid having panic attacks, such as avoidance of exercise or unfamiliar situations).

2. The panic attacks are not restricted to the direct physiological effects of a substance (e.g., a drug of abuse, a medication) or a general medical condition (e.g., hyperthyroidism, cardiopulmonary disorders).

3. The panic attacks are not restricted to the symptoms of another mental disorder, such as social phobia (e.g., in response to feared social situations), specific phobia (e.g., in response to a circumscribed phobic object or situation), obsessive-compulsive disorder (e.g., in response to dirt in someone with an obsession about contamination), post-traumatic stress disorder (e.g., in response to stimuli associated with a traumatic event), or separation anxiety disorder (e.g., in response to being away from home or close relatives).

Due to this criteria, it is essential that the clinician gather a full family mental health history. It is also important to rule out any medical issues that may be impacting the disorder, and thus a medical work-up should be scheduled to rule out any further issues. Be aware that due to the nature of panic disorder, it can also mask further disorders and so we should frequently reevaluate the patient's needs and be aware of any new symptoms that might present themselves. The best part about this diagnosis is that it is fairly straightforward: As long as the symptoms persist, we can feel comfortable with the diagnosis going forward.

As we reviewed earlier in the children's section of this chapter, it is imperative you work with your patient to help him or her identify treatment goals. This not only allows the child greater buy-in for treatment but also improves internal locus of control, as the patient can be reminded that he or she picked a goal and is actively working on it daily. What a great way to boost the self-confidence of an anxious child! Once the child has completed Jumpy's Goals for Feeling Better worksheet, you can use the goals they picked to write up your treatment plan. Let's walk through it:

Let's say your patient selected "feeling calm," "sleeping better," and "no tummy

Sample Panic Disorder Treatment Plan

Goals: Increase patient's understanding of panic disorder including symptoms and interventions. Improve somatic complaints and overall sleep patterns.

Objective One: Describe both current and past experiences with worry and panic symptoms, complete with attempted interventions and results. Verbalize an understanding of the cognitive, physiological, and behavioral components of anxiety and its treatment. Learn and implement calming skills to reduce overall anxiety and manage anxiety symptoms.

Objective Two: Define one's own state of calm including the emotional, physical, and mental aspects of same. Learn three new ways to improve personal calm through mindfulness meditation, kinetic activities, and/or sensory experiences.

Objective Three: Engage in psychoeducation regarding the gastrointestinal system. Develop an understanding of how anxiety causes or exacerbates stomach upset. Verbalize an understanding of other things that can cause stomach distress. Report 50% diminished stomach upset.

aches" on the worksheet. We can simply convert this into a treatment plan like so.
This treatment plan is simple and to the point. It addresses what the patient wants to accomplish and explains how we hope to do so. I find it helpful to work with the patient actively in treatment planning so they understand exactly what we are working toward during the course of treatment.

In the children's section we stressed that fear is automatic, and we know this is a product of our unique neurobiology. This is due to the extremely quick action of the amygdala, the fear center of the brain. It is important to emphasize the automatic nature of the amygdala as patients sometimes feel shame about what they fear. If this is the case, work on reality-testing that belief and also help them to weigh the pros and cons of self-shaming when trying to recover from the experience of panic. Stress that fear is an individual feeling; what worries one person may not worry another, and vice versa.

Chapter

8

PHOBOS, THE DRAGON OF FEAR

Phobos is so excited! His friends are all planning a trip to Dragon Springs! They are planning a fun day of playing volleyball, building sand castles, and swimming in the warm water. He was all set to pack his bags when Ember mentioned that Dragon Springs is full of sharks!

Phobos

Ever since then, Phobos not only doesn't want to go to Dragon Springs, he also doesn't want to even *think* about going. The idea of being eaten by a shark is all Phobos can think about. He can't stop thinking about sharks. He is having nightmares of sharks! He doesn't want to think about looking at a picture of a shark and he definitely doesn't want to talk about sharks. And don't even get him started on shark week! So many sharks, with their rows and rows and rows of teeth...

Initially, Phobos felt safe as long as he wasn't going to the beach. But then he started to worry about whether sharks might get into his bathtub, or the shower, or anywhere water might be. Which means he stopped bathing... with obvious effects!

Phobos's friends knew that something was wrong, but there was no convincing him that he was safe. They pointed out that sharks cannot live in his bathtub or his shower, but he wouldn't listen. They told him that Dragon Springs is too warm for a shark, and there has never even been a shark sighting there, but he disagreed. They even convinced their science teacher, Mrs. Quizenberry, to review sharks in class but that ended disastrously.

Phobos was even worse after the incident in science class. Why would his friends do that to him? Didn't they understand the danger they were all in? He set about making himself a shark safety kit and rigged up booby traps in his bathroom just in case a shark did try to get in there.

Phobos's little brother, Tanzit, found his behavior quite peculiar. He looked up to his big brother and wanted to be just like him when he grew up. But his odd fear of the water was really starting to cause trouble in the household... and at school!

For one thing, Phobos refused to go with the family to Dragon Springs. Tanzit and Phobos had made a fort there one summer and it was one of Tanzit's favorite places to play.

Suddenly, though, Phobos seemed to want nothing to do with their fort, or with him, for that matter. He refused to watch Tanzit's swim team practice and because he wouldn't travel far from the house, the family was unable to go hiking or sight-seeing. He never asked Tanzit about his team practices and spent most of his time in his room alone, with the door closed.

At first, Tanzit was really angry at his brother for being so selfish. But then he began to wonder, had *he* done something to upset Phobos? Was he a bad brother? What could he have done wrong to make his brother not love him anymore? The thought of it made him so upset he started to cry.

Tanzit knew he needed to apologize to his brother for whatever he had done to make him hate him so much. So he decided to write him a quick note. Once he was finished, he slid it under Phobos's door.

When Phobos read the note, he felt like he was going to cry. Why did Tanzit think he hated him? He had to go talk to him.

"Tanzit!" Phobos began. "Why did you write that note? You know I don't hate you, right?"

"Then why won't you talk with me or play with me? Why don't you go to swim practice?" Tanzit asked.

"That's not because of you," Phobos began, taking his brother into his lap. "That's because of me. It's because I'm... scared of things."

"Scared?" Tanzit said. "You aren't scared of anything. You're the bravest brother in the whole world!"

"I'm really not," Phobos said sadly. "I'm afraid of... sharks."

Tanzit let out a great big laugh. "What?! No you're not! You are stronger than a shark, and faster. You can breathe fire!"

"But Tanzit," Phobos said, "They have rows and rows of teeth. They can bite you and chew you up."

"Pfft!" said Tanzit in disbelief. "They can't bite what they can't catch. Anyway, there are no sharks here. They can't get here because there is no ocean to connect to. I'm only in kindergarten and I know that! And even if they did, you are the smartest, bravest brother in the whole wide world! You would protect me and everyone else."

Phobos looked at his brother and how he seemed so sure of himself. "You really think I could protect you?"

"Remember that time I was afraid of the bambuds in the Forgetful Forest? Why, you caught one yourself, just to show me that they were harmless. You are my hero!"

Phobos *did* remember. He felt so proud of that moment, and he was glad it meant something to Tanzit as well.

"Phobos, I can't go to my swim meet without you. Please! I'm so scared! It's my first ever swim meet, and I know I can be brave if you are there. Please?"

Phobos saw the hope in Tanzit's eyes and he knew he needed to make a change. "Don't worry, Tanzit. I will be there for you!" As Tanzit skipped away happily, Phobos added, "Somehow..."

Phobos figured the only way he could get past his fear would be magic. Surely there was a potion or elixir that could make him brave enough to attend the swim meet. After school he decided to go visit Mama Gumbo.

"Mama Gumbo... umm... I need your help," Phobos said quietly.

"Ah, Phobos, is it? I am happy to help you. What do you need? A birthday tart? A special side dish for dinner?"

"It's... magical," Phobos said.

"Oh... I see." Mama Gumbo ushered Phobos to a small room in the back of her place, away from the customers who were all enjoying a wonderful meal. "And what is bothering you, youngling?"

Phobos explained that he needed a cure for his fear of sharks. He told Mama Gumbo all about how it started and noted that he had found himself feeling more and more afraid of anything related to sharks. Even water was upsetting to him. He added ruefully, "It's ruining my life."

Mama Gumbo truly felt for Phobos. "I can help you, Phobos," she began, selecting some items from her special cabinet. "But I will need you to tell me more to make the potion work best."

Phobos agreed to help her.

"What is the worst part of the shark for you?" Mama Gumbo asked, mixing some powders in a large bowl.

Phobos explained that he didn't like its eyes or its teeth. "It has rows and rows of teeth! Can you believe it? Why does it need so many teeth? I'll tell you why! TO EAT YOU!"

Mama Gumbo asked him to draw a picture of the scariest shark he could think of for her to study while she continued to decide on ingredients. Phobos admitted it was hard for him to do so, but he would try.

Mama Gumbo then explained that she and Phobos would need to imagine him coming across a shark just like the one he drew. Phobos told her that was too scary, so she asked him if there was something he could think of that made him feel safe.

Phobos remembered that whenever he thinks of his pet bird, Tweetsie, he feels much better. "She's the best bird ever!"

Mama Gumbo asked him again to think of coming across the shark, but this time to also imagine his little bird with him. She also suggested that instead of being afraid, he understand that it is imaginary and cannot hurt him. She asked him to imagine being near the shark if there was no danger.

She told him that in order for the potion to work, he would need to imagine this a few times a day, each time getting closer to the shark while understanding he is safe. She explained that each time he did so, he would need to take three deep breaths, in through his nose and out through his mouth before and after. Phobos readily agreed.

"Mama Gumbo," Phobos began, "I might be able to feel safe when I imagine the shark, but I wouldn't be, not in real life."

"That may be true," said Mama Gumbo, "but if you actually did come across a shark, wouldn't you want to be calm and make the right choices? Imagine if Tanzit swam near a shark. If you panicked, you wouldn't be able to help him. If you were calm, you could get him away from the shark and save you both! Imagine how wonderful *that* would feel! You would be a hero!"

Phobos felt a wave of warmth passing over him. He would do anything to protect his brother. He had to brave!

"Here you are," said Mama Gumbo, handing Phobos a small bottle. "When you need to feel brave, just imagine being near that shark, feel yourself being brave, and take a small sip. The potion will bring you courage."

Phobos was so relieved! He put the potion into his pocket and hurried home, excited to finally be free of his fear.

Phobos announced to his family that he planned to attend his brother's swim meet and his parents were delighted, if not a little surprised by this sudden change of heart. Phobos remembered what Mama Gumbo had said about imagining himself with the shark and did so every single day, typically at least three times.

As the day of the swim meet grew closer, Phobos's friends noticed he was less nervous and more fun to be around. His parents noticed he was eating better and sleeping more soundly. He was more patient with his brother and his school work was improving. All because of Mama Gumbo's potion!

The day of the swim meet began bright and sunny. Tanzit was so excited! He asked Phobos to come with him to warm up. They had just called the swimmers to their places when Tanzit froze in place.

"Tanzit, what's the matter?" Phobos asked.

"I'm scared!" Tanzit said tearfully. "I don't know if I can do it!" He clutched his brother closely and cried.

Phobos hugged his brother close and noticed the potion in his pocket. If it worked for him, why couldn't it work for Tanzit?

"Tanzit," Phobos whispered, "I have a way to make you brave, but you have to do exactly what I say, okay?"

"Really?" Tanzit asked, eyes wide.

Phobos instructed Tanzit to take three deep, slow breaths. He then told him to imagine himself doing well in the meet. Tanzit began to smile.

"Tell me what it would feel like to know you were really successful at the meet," said Phobos.

A big smile spread across Tanzit's face. He described feeling proud, and knowing he had done his best.

Phobos took out the potion and realized he was down to his last few sips. For a brief second, Phobos considered keeping the potion just to himself. But then he looked at Tanzit's tear-stained face, beaming with hope. He smiled and passed the potion to Tanzit. Tanzit drank it quickly, then ran to get into place for the meet.

And what a meet it was! Tanzit was amazing! He shocked everyone by coming in first in the freestyle category, and his team placed second overall. He was so very proud.

As he received his trophy, he beamed at his brother. He knew Phobos had saved him. His family rushed up to congratulate him.

Among his well-wishers was Mama Gumbo.

"I am so proud of you, Tanzit! I guess bravery runs in your family." She winked at Phobos as she started to make her way to the exit.

Phobos ran after her. "Mama Gumbo! I... I did a bad thing." Mama Gumbo stopped to give him her full attention. "I gave Tanzit the last of the potion. I wanted him to feel brave and he did, he did! But now I am all out, and I need more." He handed the bottle to her.

Mama Gumbo let out a kind laugh. "Oh, dear Phobos. You don't need it anymore. It is inside you now. All you have to do in the future to be brave is to take your breaths, imagine the scary situation, and see yourself succeeding. And now you have shared this gift with your brother, how wonderful! I am so proud of you, Phobos. You conquered your fear and you helped your brother to boot! You *are* a hero!"

Phobos grinned from ear to ear. She was right; he *did* feel the courage inside him! He ran back to his family, waving to Mama Gumbo as he did.

Mama Gumbo went to find the General so they could begin their walk home.

"So, what did you use this time?" the General asked with a smile. She handed him the little bottle. The General took a quick sniff. "Orange soda?"

Mama Gumbo let out a giggle. "With just a touch of lemon." She and the General began out into the sun-soaked courtyard. "The power has been inside him all along, and he helped his brother."

"Sounds like we have a budding potion master," the General laughed.

Poor Phobos! What a tough time he had. Have you ever felt scared of something like Phobos? Let's think about how Mama Gumbo fixed the problem. The first step is to take nice, deep breaths to help you calm your body down. The next step is to imagine the scary thing, and you can also add in something that makes you feel safe if that helps. Finish up with some more deep breaths. Remember: deep breaths help your body calm down and relax you. They are so very good for you! Then you need to do that every day, and each day it will get better. Sometimes people decide to go ahead and actually be near the scary thing, but that's something you and a trusted adult need to decide. Go slow, and you will get it over time.

Just a couple of quick tips: Make sure that while you are working on your fears you try to keep yourself relaxed and don't expose yourself to other scary things, like movies or television shows. No need to stress yourself out! You also want to avoid caffeine, something that is found in coffee, certain sodas, and energy drinks, because it can make you feel more anxious.

Keep it up, and you can be a hero, just like Phobos!

Phobias

Phobias can be very tricky to treat, as sometimes people feel so upset by the phobia they don't know where to start. A phobia is defined as a strong or irrational fear that poses little or no actual danger. They can be specific or general, and it is typical for the sufferer to want to avoid the thing they are afraid of. In their quest to stay away from the feared item/event, they have to engage in increasingly avoidant behaviors that lead to other fearful actions and increasing anxiety, oftentimes impacting sleep, appetite, and overall anxiety.

When assessing a phobia, first you have to determine whether or not the child can call the phobia by a name. Some fears are so scary you cannot say them out loud. In that case, you may have to decide on a word that indicates the fear.

You will then need to create a fear hierarchy—and don't worry, it's not as tough as it sounds. Mama Gumbo did that this by asking Phobos to draw the shark and then explain what the *worst* parts of being around the shark are. When we build a hierarchy, we figure out the worst part first and then what the child can tolerate. For example, the child might say they cannot handle looking at a real, live shark, but can better tolerate a picture of a shark. You might then want to see if they can tolerate a representation of a shark, such as a stuffed animal or drawing. Keep working with the child until you find something he or she can tolerate well. You will then work on exposing the child to that thought, just as Mama Gumbo had Phobos imagine himself with his bird near the shark. She had him engage in mindful breathing before and after his imaginary exposure and stressed the need for ongoing practice so as to improve his responses to the stimuli.

Ideally, once the child has mastered one level of the hierarchy you would present the next level and so on. In the meantime, you want to increase activities the child finds relaxing and decrease exposure to upsetting stimuli. I am also very stern about keeping the child away from caffeine. Stimulants are a big no-no for anxious kids!

Here is an example of a potential treatment plan. We'll use Phobos as our patient.

Sample Phobia Treatment Plan

Goal: Phobos will exhibit a decrease in overall anxiety as evidenced by improvement in sleep, appetite, and frustration tolerance. Additionally, Phobos will demonstrate a reduction in psychomotor agitation related to the phobic event or object.

Objective One: Phobos will learn episodic deep breathing to improve overall experience of anxiety. Phobos will practice deep breathing at least once daily. Phobos agrees to engage in physical activity three times weekly to manage the kinetic needs of his anxiety at this time.

Objective Two: Phobos will work in session and at home to engage in imaginary exposure to the feared stimuli. Phobos will work with his team to create an image or script to create imaginary exposure and will complete deep breathing exercises prior to and following these events.

Objective Three: Phobos will build a fear hierarchy and work with his team to begin working on actual exposure to the levels of his hierarchy. Phobos will attain mastery of the base of his hierarchy prior to moving forward in the hierarchy, meaning he will demonstrate ability to be exposed to the item in the hierarchy without significant anxious response.

Just a final word on phobias: I think it's important to understand that there are certain fears expected of children dependent on age. For example, children under the age of two are expected to be afraid of loud noises as well as strangers and being separated from their parents. Elementary schoolers and pre-teens tend to be afraid of imaginary things, like ghosts and monsters, while older children are afraid of more normalized fears, like death, rejection, or isolation. It's important in treatment that the family works to help normalize the experience of fear as well as being clear that everyone gets scared sometimes. Remind kids that fears can be conquered, and we are all here to help them be brave.

WEEPY, THE DRAGON OF LONELINESS

"WaaaAaaaaAaaaaa!"

Every morning, Weepy's dad heard the same noise whenever he got ready to leave his little daughter, Weepy, at preschool.

Weepy

It seemed like no matter what he tried, she just got more and more upset whenever he dropped her off. The preschool workers assured him that Weepy would get used to it and start to cry less, but it broke his heart to leave her. Still, he had to go to work so he could take good care of her, so despite how sad it made him he had to leave.

For her part, Weepy was getting louder and louder still! She was so upset that her daddy was leaving. Why was he going away? And who were these weird people anyway? She didn't want to play with them, or sing, or even eat lunch. She wanted her daddy!

Sometimes she would throw herself on the floor and kick her legs while she cried and punched. It got really bad one day when she let out a little fire spark and almost took out the kitchen!

The preschool workers were at their wit's end—what could they do to help Weepy to feel better about staying with them?

They decided to consult with Dr. Prudens first to make sure there was nothing wrong with her.

After a thorough examination, it was determined that Weepy was just fine.

"Well," concluded Dr. Prudens, "it's nothing physical, which means it's emotional." He went into his drawer to find a pen and instead pulled out a small bear.

Weepy became very excited, reaching for the bear. This gave the doctor an idea.

"Nurse, get me another bear... and a smaller bear. I think I know just what to do." The nurse did as she was asked and soon they had two new bears to work with.

"Okay," began the doctor, "Weepy, I want you to hold this baby bear, and dad, you hold this papa bear. Now I want you both to hug those bears! Give them lots and lots of love. I want you to think about how much you love each other, and put all that love into those bears. Whisper the nice things you say to each other into the bears, and give them loads of kisses. Now if either of you want to decorate your bears, that's fine, too. But first, I need to tell them something." He whispered something to each bear and then yelled, "Alakazam!"

"And there you go," Dr. Prudens said. "Now I have added the final element: a bring-back spell. Weepy, whenever you go to preschool, you and Dad are going to exchange bears. Daddy will get the baby bear, which is yours, and you will get the papa bear, which is Daddy's. Since you two have each other's bears, you will always come back together at the end of the day. And anytime you feel like you miss each other, you can hug their bear and know wherever they are, they can feel that hug and know you love them very much. What do you think?"

Weepy was overjoyed! Now she had a part of her daddy all the time. He would always know when she missed him and she could hug him, even when he wasn't there. What a great idea!

"Now be very careful with your bears," cautioned the doctor. "You don't want to lose them. But if you do, we can make another one. I know it is hard to be away from someone you love very much, but this will make it easier."

They thanked the good doctor and agreed to try. He warned them it might be hard at first, but if they kept practicing it would get better. He also encouraged them to reward themselves with special time for just the two of them whenever Weepy did a good job letting Daddy leave for work.

With a little bit of practice, Weepy was much better at going to preschool, and they started a brand new tradition of going for walks in the forest after school and playing their favorite games. Weepy was so happy to be with her daddy but found out she could have fun with her new friends at preschool, too!

Have you ever felt like Weepy? It is very hard to be separated from the people we love, especially when we are very young. Did you know adults and even animals have problems with this, too? My nerfle, Cleo, was so upset when I went over to spend the night at my best friend's house, my mom said she cried all night and wouldn't sleep!

I find it helps me to think about what will most likely happen rather than what I worry about. For example, I worry my mom won't come and pick me up after school, but then I remember she has never once forgotten me in the past and that she always picks me up. Even if she couldn't pick me up, she would have my dad or grandma get me and then she would be home later. Try to do this type of thinking with your worries. When you remember what generally happens, it helps to calm down these types of worries.

Sometimes when we aren't with the people we love, we worry about them. Does that ever happen to you? What kind of worries do you have about them? On the next page are some worries I have when my mom is away at work.

MY WORRY LIST

Anybody can have the worries! It helps to write them down or draw them so we know what bothers us. Try that here:

I worry that when my mom is away at work she won't come home!!!!!

Now, let's come up with a way to fix our worry! Pretend you can fix it any way you like. You can write it down or draw a picture. Be creative and I bet we can find a great solution!

I would make a magical crystal ball where I could see my mom no matter where she was! And she could hear me through it, so we could talk all the time. Finally, I could also use it to transport her wherever I am instantly. It would be so cool!!!

MY WORRY LIST

Anybody can have the worries! It helps to write them down or draw them so we know what bothers us. Try that here:

Now, let's come up with a way to fix our worry! Pretend that you can fix it any way you like. You can write it down or draw a picture. Be creative and I bet we can find a great solution!

Separation Anxiety

Separation anxiety is defined as excessive anxiety associated with being separated or anticipating being separated from a loved one. It can impact anyone, even adults! It is a very normal part of childhood, but needs to be handled quickly and consistently in order to help the child become more independent and allow the child to separate more positively in the future.

One of the first things you need to do is to gauge the child's age as well as how he or she has handled separations in the past, if any. For an example, a child who is facing their first separation at the age of six will handle this much differently than a four-year-old who has experienced regular separations since they were three. In terms of child development, age leads to different understandings of the child's relationship to caregivers. Below is a quick overview of the major times of attachment:

6 months and younger: Begins to develop relationships with others, demonstrated by playing peek-a-boo and other attentional games.

7 to 9 months: Attachment develops and the child begins to notice whenever the primary caregiver is missing. This results in emotional pain and the child will exhibit severe stress.

15 to 18 months: The child begins to develop what is called a "secure base," meaning the child feels safe with certain caregivers but when in an unfamiliar environment or around strange people, the child will cling to the caregiver for safety.

2½ to 3 years: This is the stage when children develop "negotiation of separation." This means that when the child anticipates separation, he or she will attempt to negotiate more time with the loved one. For example, the child might ask for one more hug, one more story, or one more drink of water just to keep the caregiver in their area.

If the child moves through these stages well, they will be able to separate appropriately by the age of three with occasional retraining necessary when encountering new situations or stimuli. This tends to continue up and through first grade, as going to school is a significant change for children and creates an entirely new day structure.

When you need to create a separation plan, it is important that you first speak with the caregivers about any trepidation they may have in regard to the separation. Children tend to pick up on the emotions of their caregivers and if the caregiver is not committed to the separation the child may recognize this and become more anxious.

Specifically, you need to address if there are any issues within the family in regard to loss, such as a miscarriage. Further, you need to rule out family violence, addiction, and other mental health disorders, as these can make it much harder to separate. Remember, all behavior has meaning!

Once everyone is on board, we need to create a clear and consistent separation plan to put in place. It needs to be clear and concise, and everyone involved needs to know what the plan entails and be able to consistently fulfill their part of the plan. Let's take a look at how we create a separation plan.

Sample Separation Treatment Plan

Separation plans are easier than you think! Here are the key points:

- Teach the child relaxation techniques to aid with overall anxiety. Practice this with all participants.

- Practice the separation in tiny increments first. Initially, you can do it without anyone leaving, then allow the caregiver to leave the room, then the house, then the yard, until you are ready to try it in the real space.

- Schedule separations after nap times and feedings. Cranky, tired people do *not* separate well.

- Develop a "goodbye ritual." Say goodbye, have a specific action to denote affection, and decide whatever else you need to do to let each other know the goodbye is happening. Remember Dr. Prudens!

- Keep the surroundings familiar. Always separate in the same space, if possible. If you have to use a new space, make it as familiar as possible.

- Have a consistent caregiver who remains with the child after the separation.

- Leave without fanfare. Smothering a child with kisses makes it much harder to separate appropriately.

- Minimize exposure to scary media.

- Encourage the caregiver not to give up and not to give in. Change takes practice!

A growing concern apart from separation anxiety is school refusal. Current statistics suggest that when left untreated, as many as 50% of those refusing school will not graduate from high school, predicting loss of gainful employment and suitable income for adulthood.

The key to treating school refusal is establishing the *reason* for the refusal. I always remind my patients that my job is to solve problems and I cannot solve a problem that is not defined. Just as I cannot write an excuse note without a reason, I cannot work on school refusals unless I know why it is occurring.

These are typical causes of school refusal:

1. Inappropriate academic placement
2. Avoidance of school due to fear of violence or teasing
3. Conduct disorder
4. Substance abuse or dependence
5. Depression
6. Grief reaction
7. Brain tumor (especially if associated with vision or coordination impairment)
8. Communication disorder
9. Cultural issues

Please understand: This list is by no means exhaustive, but lists many of the primary causes of school refusal. Once you have ascertained the reason for the refusal, you need to work with the patient and family to assess your next course of action. Typically, contacting the school and scheduling a meeting with the patient's teachers and/or administration is helpful to begin monitoring and improving the situation.

Sometimes it is important to also speak with peers, as they may be more aware of peer relationships and potential covert bullying. Once you know what the cause is, I typically suggest identifying a safe place in the school for the child to check in upon entering school as well as when they are upset. Work on tools they can use during the school day to manage anxiety and see if there is a need to accommodate late arrivals or early departures initially if this will at least allow the child to make it into school daily.

Sample Separation Anxiety Treatment Plan

Goal: Work on tolerating separation from the identified attachment figure(s) without exhibiting (insert the specific symptoms here, such as: heightened emotional distress, regressive behaviors, temper outbursts, or pleading).

Objective One: Child will be able to describe the fear and specific triggers that tend to make this intensify. Verbally identify family dynamics or stressors that contribute to feelings of anxiety. Express feelings and fears in play therapy, mutual storytelling, and art.

Objective Two: Parents/caregivers will work to establish and maintain appropriate parent-child boundaries and set firm, consistent limits with the child. Parents/caregivers will work with therapist to identify times that the child demonstrates temper outbursts or manipulative behaviors. Parents/caregivers will reinforce the child's autonomous behavior and set limits on overly dependent behaviors.

Objective Three: Child will work on learning assertive behaviors to deal more effectively and directly with stress. Child will work on conflict resolution skills as well as frustration tolerance skills. The child will work on participating in extracurricular or peer group activities and spend time in independent play on a regular, consistent basis.

Finally, always acknowledge all good efforts in separation or school refusal. A kind word can go a long way in helping someone to conquer their fears and grow!

MONOS, THE SOCIALLY ANXIOUS DRAGON

Wow, it is a really busy day in Longwei because it's time for the annual Harvest Fair! It is great fun. Everyone carves pumpkins and sings songs until the early morning. That's where I learned how to make smoke rings and fireworks out of my dragon fire! Everybody looks so happy!

But wait—who is that over there? See him, waaay in the back corner? Oh, no! I think that might be Monos! You've probably never heard of him, but Monos used to be one of the most popular dragons around. But now he just hides in corners, mumbling to himself. To understand what happened, we need to go back a few years.

What do you think of his yearbook photograph from Longwei Middle School? Go Raiders! As you can see from this picture, Monos is a pretty happy guy. He is funny, smart, and has lots of friends. He's good in school and plays two different sports. That all changed the day he lost his favorite necklace.

Monos

You see, when Monos was just a youngling his great-grandpa, Pop-pop, gave him a special necklace: an amulet that was passed down from generation to generation in his family.

"This was given to me by my great-granddaddy and his great granddaddy before him," said Pop-pop.

Monos stared in wonder at the necklace. He had never seen his Pop-pop without it.

Pop-pop continued, "Monos, this is a mystical amulet! Anyone who wears it will be gifted with courage, intelligence, and friendship. Wear this and nothing can ever hurt you!"

Monos wore that amulet proudly everywhere he went (even in the shower!) and there was no time he relied on it more than the night of the big basketball championship. His team, the Raiders, was facing their rivals, the Vikings. They just had to win, they just *had* to!

The fourth quarter was quickly ending and the clock showed it all came down to this one moment. Five seconds left on the clock and Monos had to make the free throw or they would lose the game. There was so much pressure! Still, he knew he could do it with the help of his trusty amulet.

"Hey, buddy, your shoe's untied," his friend Rocco said.

"Thanks!" Monos knelt down to tie his shoe. Unfortunately, the referee accidentally stumbled into him, knocking his amulet to the floor and breaking it. CRASH!

Monos stared in disbelief. He couldn't believe what had happened. Everything switched to slow motion. Monos could hear people talking to him but couldn't make out their words. His coach was waving his arms at him, but Monos sat perfectly still on the floor, clutching the broken pieces of his amulet to his chest.

What happened next was like a dream—a terrible, miserable dream. Monos sat like a statue on the floor while the game clock timed out. The buzzer screamed! The game was over, and the Raiders had lost the championship. All because of Monos. Monos and his now-broken amulet.

Understandably, Monos was a mess after the game. He was ashamed about what had happened and didn't feel like he could do anything without his amulet. He was so upset that he had broken it. It was a family heirloom! His father was always telling him to be careful with his things, and he irresponsibly broke it, right when it mattered the most! He had single-handedly doomed his entire family to a luckless life because he had stupidly broken the amulet! He couldn't stop crying.

Monos felt too upset to go to school and his mom let him take a few days off. His friends even came by to visit but he was too ashamed to speak with them. *They must think I am such an idiot!* Monos thought. *How could I let this happen?* He hid under his covers and tried to fade into nothingness.

After a week his mother and father insisted he return to school. They thought it would help him feel better if he could see his friends and teachers and return to a place that gave him such joy. Monos's friends were surprised to see him, but happy, too. Unfortunately, when Monos saw their expressions he thought he could read their minds. And what he read wasn't good!

They think I'm a loser, he thought. *They see what a joke I am.*

Monos started to pull away from his friends. He was so worried people would make fun of him he started to avoid them altogether. He quit his sports teams and stopped speaking up in class. Soon he started wearing a cloak to cover himself and he spent all of his free time alone.

One day Monos's mom needed to go by Mama Gumbo's for some spices and although she usually left Monos at home, their house was being painted so she felt it was best he come with her.

Monos pleaded with her to let him stay home, but his mother insisted. Begrudgingly he pulled on his shoes and followed his mother to the store.

He was surprised to see the dazzling array of items in Mama Gumbo's inventory. She had spices, tarts, and other baked goods. She also had several trinkets and gifts for visitors. He looked through one of the glass display cases and couldn't believe his eyes—what was that? Way in the back, Monos saw a shiny object. He looked closer and was amazed to see his amulet!

"Excuse me?" Monos asked. "Excuse me! I must have that amulet!" He started waving and pointing frantically.

"What?" asked Mama Gumbo. "You mean this amulet? This one right here?"

She carefully removed it from the case and placed it in Monos's hands. Instantly, Monos felt a rush of self-confidence. It was working! He absolutely *had* to have that amulet. "Yes, this is the one! I must have it! I'll pay whatever you want!"

Mama Gumbo chuckled quietly. "Youngling, this amulet here? I got it from right over there." She pointed to a coin machine full of identical amulets, all on sale for one Kupi. "I just thought it would look nice in the display case, so I added it in. Gives it some class, don't you think?"

Monos rushed to the machine, Mama Gumbo right behind him. "But how is this possible? My Pop-pop gave it to me when I was really little. It means a lot to my family!"

"I don't know what you've been told, Monos, but these here are junk!"

"But my great granddaddy Silas—"

"Silas?" Mama Gumbo let out a throaty laugh. "Oh, what a hoot! He is such a trickster! He would come by all the time, loved my maple candies. So what, he bought this for you?"

"He told me it had magical powers, and it would make me brave and smart... but then it broke." Monos looked sadly at her.

"Well, no wonder. It's only worth one Kupi. You get what you pay for."

"But its magic made me so amazing, and when it broke, I turned into... this." Monos gestured at himself with tears in his eyes.

Mama Gumbo gave him a hug. "Youngling, there's no magic in this silly piece of jewelry. Anything you accomplished you did on your own, because you are YOU. That is all." She put some money into the machine and popped out a brand new amulet. "Here you are. You want more, you can buy one here anytime. But it won't change who you are. A necklace can't change the good person you are. Silas probably just wanted you to feel a little more confident. He always would brag about how proud he is of you. I hear you're a pretty amazing student, and a great sports guy."

"A great sports guy who lost the championship basketball game," Monos said sadly.

"Your *team* lost," Mama corrected. "You all lost together. You win together, you lose together; that is what a team is. In any game, there are winners and losers. So, it wasn't the Raider's night, so what? You are still a great person. Don't let one action define you. Did you know that when I first tried to bake, I was absolutely horrible at it? I almost burned down my grandmother's hut! But I didn't let that stop me. I tried again and again, and I got better at it. Listen, there is a whole big world out there. You have to stop avoiding it! Play with friends, go to birthday parties. Play basketball! That is what Silas would want for you." She gave him another hug.

Monos's mother was surprised to see her son hugging Mama Gumbo. He had been keeping to himself for such a long time! But after that day, something changed. Monos started to return to himself. He started spending time with friends and rejoined the basketball team. He was surprised to find that the only person who seemed to hold the championship game against him was himself.

His amulet now sits in a space of honor in his room, right above his bed. It lets him know great granddaddy is looking over him and reminds him that being a good person comes from inside. And that makes him smile!

Have you ever had something embarrassing happen to you and, like Monos, pulled yourself away from the people who care about you? Sometimes we start to fear how people will respond to us and worry they are thinking badly of us. When that happens, you may find yourself avoiding others and keeping to yourself. If you're not careful, you may end up pushing away people who really care about you!

Let's talk about the people in your life who make you feel the most comfortable. Here in Longwei, we call them "Anchors," because just like an anchor keeps a boat safe and grounded, these people help us feel safe and comfortable. I will do one and then you, okay?

ANCHORS AHOY!

In the dragon village of Longwei, an "anchor" is someone who helps you feel safe and grounded. They are really important because they are there for us whether we are happy, sad, or whatever! It's important to know who you feel safe with to help balance out unsafe feelings from people you fear.

Here are the names of people I consider to be my anchors:

My mommy

Daddy

Granny

My best friend, Shalla

My nerfle, Cleo

My art teacher, Mrs. Farris

When I am around my anchors I feel like this: (you can write down your answer or draw it)

Happy

Safe

Loved

Relaxed

Warm

Here is my plan to see one of my anchors soon:

I get to see my parents and Granny every day. I see Shalla at school and hiker's club. I play with Cleo as much as I can and snuggle her at night. I get to see Mrs. Farris whenever I have art class.

ANCHORS AHOY!

In the dragon village of Longwei, an "anchor" is someone who helps you to feel safe and grounded. They are really important, because they are there for us whether we are happy, sad, or whatever! It's important to know who you feel safe with to help balance out unsafe feelings from people you fear.

Here are the names of people I consider to be my anchors:

When I am around my anchors I feel like this: (you can write down your answer or draw it)

Here is my plan to see one of my anchors soon:

HELPER SECTION

Social Anxiety

Social anxiety disorder is a growing concern in our world as the advent of the internet age makes it easier and easier for us to avoid interacting with each other. It is important to treat social anxiety disorder in a timely fashion, as it can generalize over time into more significant anxiety and even agoraphobia (a fear of open spaces that tends to make people afraid to leave their homes). Let's examine which symptoms compose social anxiety disorder. The following criteria are taken from the *DSM-5®(Diagnostic and Statistical Manual of Mental Disorders, fifth edition)*:

1. A persistent fear of one or more social or performance situations in which the person is exposed to unfamiliar people or to possible scrutiny by others. The individual fears that he or she will act in a way (or show anxiety symptoms) that will be embarrassing and humiliating.

2. Exposure to the feared situation almost invariably provokes anxiety, which may take the form of a situationally-bound or situationally pre-disposed panic attack.

3. The person recognizes that this fear is unreasonable or excessive.

4. The feared situations are avoided or else are endured with intense anxiety and distress.

5. The avoidance, anxious anticipation, or distress in the feared social or performance situation(s) interferes significantly with the person's normal routine, occupational (academic) functioning, or social activities or relationships, or there is marked distress about having the phobia.

6. The fear, anxiety, or avoidance is persistent, typically lasting six or more months.

7. The fear or avoidance is not due to direct physiological effects of a substance (e.g., drugs, medications) or a general medical condition not better accounted for by another mental disorder. (American Psychiatric Association, 2013.)

As you can see, there are a lot of rule-outs when dealing with social anxiety disorder, so it is important to have the child medically cleared prior to developing the diagnosis. Once the diagnosis has been given, the treatment plan should focus on establishing baseline behaviors and then working on improving responses to social situations.

Sample Social Anxiety Treatment Plan

Goal: Patient will improve ability to be exposed to both known and unknown social situations demonstrated by reduction in anxiety symptoms such as reduced heart rate, decrease in panic attacks by 25%, improvement in sleep, and reduction in (specify any clear symptoms that impact the child here).

Objective One: Patient will work on developing rapport with clinician through play therapy, music therapy, and talk therapy. Patient will identify people in his or her life who are considered safe and can be interacted with easily.

Objective Two: Patient will resume regular school attendance. Caregivers will communicate with the school in regard to any deficit areas and work to maintain appropriate grade placement.

Objective Three: Patient will work to create location goals and new people goals to allow him or her to continue to nurture socialization skills. Patient will create new goals during weekly therapy and complete regular anxiety logs to create accounts of measurable progress.

A quick word: Before delving into treatment, it is important to assess the child's socialization skills. Does the child make eye contact? Does the child have appropriate physical boundaries with others? Do they understand pitch and tone, as well as nuanced speech (such as sarcasm)? It is important to assess this as deficits in these skills can lead a child to being left out of social interactions with others. You also want to work hard on managing body symptoms and reviewing anxiety logs (both can be found in Chapter 5) so they have a strong foundation to work from.

I find that during my early work with these lovely children, we spend most of our time building rapport, and I get to really know these exceptional people. This helps me to pinpoint any socialization skills that may be lacking and help them to learn new skills that will open them up to the amazing social opportunities our world can present.

Chapter 11

MUTOS, THE QUIET DRAGON

Do you hear that? Silence! Silence in the whispering woods! That can mean only one thing: Mutos must be around!

Mutos is a legend around here. The story goes that Mutos had a lovely singing voice, quite possibly the most beautiful voice ever heard in our village of Longwei. It was said her voice was so sweet, it could call the great grackles off of Tolkien's Peak! Wait, you don't know about the grackles? Oh, heavens, you must!

Mutos

Grackles are beautiful, magnificent birds who make their nests high atop Tolkien's Peak. There they raise their young, who are born in beautiful, magical eggs. When grackles are born, the eggs hatch and then change into lovely gemstones that are highly prized. Typically the grackles hide them throughout the many caves on the peak, but occasionally they will favor others with a gem to thank them for food or care. The dragons in Longwei use the grackle gems as currency, and they fetch a high price when traded.

But look at me, just going on here! Anyway, Mutos was a friend of the grackles and she would oftentimes climb up on Tolkien's Peak to gaze at their amazing plumage and favor them with a song. The grackles in return might give her a gem or a ride home. Mutos always brought the gems back to her parents and looked forward to visiting her friends, high up in their nest.

Oh, do you see Ember? That rascal is hiding right off to the right in that picture, isn't he? Well, Ember is always looking to steal his way to riches, and when he heard Mutos could supply him with almost unending gems, he practically fell out of his tree! He hatched an evil plot to trick Mutos into helping him.

"I'll find that Mutos... and I'll make her sing for the grackles! Then I will steal all the gems for myself!" he laughed evilly as he began hatching his diabolical plan.

One day while Mutos was travelling through the woods, she heard a dreadful sobbing. Alarmed, she ran to see what had happened.

"Youngling! Please help me!" called an old woman with a kerchief. "I have lost my way! I live up near the top of Tolkien's Peak, and I don't know how to get home." Ember snickered to himself. His disguise was working!

Mutos attempted to explain the way to the old woman but she had difficulty understanding. As the woman was unsteady on her feet, Mutos agreed to accompany her. The grackles immediately saw Mutos approaching and they excitedly ran from their nests to hear her sing. Ember, disguised as the old woman, thanked her for her help and ran off. Mutos and the grackles enjoyed a few songs together while Ember filled his greedy pockets with grackle gems! Just as he was about to make his getaway, he woke one of the grackle babies and she started to wail.

The cave was launched into chaos! Grackles were flying, screeching, and generally making quite a noise! Mutos and her friends ran toward the thief, but they were too late. As he escaped, he yelled, "Thanks, Mutos! Couldn't have done it without you!" in his old lady voice.

Mutos was horrified. How could she have been so foolish? She had been tricked into letting a stranger into the grackles' cave.

The grackles did not understand what had happened and believed Mutos had betrayed them. Angry, they used their magic to take Mutos's beautiful singing voice and encased it in one of the jeweled eggs, and cursed her further, so whenever she is near others, they also would also be unable to speak! Because of this, the woods where she lives has been renamed the "Whispering Woods" and it is said even the wind is quiet here. Mutos has been waiting for someone to help her to break the spell so she can sing again!

Would you like to help me try to save Mutos's voice? I understand the town leaders have been working hard to try to recover Mutos's voice. They have to work far away from her for now though, because when she's around: Poof! No more voice! Doctor Prudens examined Mutos and found that there is no medical reason Mutos can't speak, so Mama Gumbo examined Mutos.

"I am familiar with grackle magic," said Mama Gumbo. "Their power only works on emotions. It seems like your shame about what happened with the grackles is keeping the magic spell intact, and keeping your voice hostage."

Because Mama Gumbo felt Mutos's emotions were stopping the spell from breaking, she figured the first thing they needed to do was to address Mutos's sadness and shame. Mama Gumbo thought Mutos had to be calm before we could really start trying to help her. So she consulted Galen to talk about using her five senses to help her calm down. Do you remember those from Chapter 5? If not, feel free to sneak a peek now! Which sense do you think Mutos would like to use? Which one is your favorite to use?

Now we need to figure out who Mutos feels the most comfortable talking to and who she feels the least comfortable talking to. Here is what she wrote down:

SAFETY SPEAK!

We all have people we feel more comfortable talking with as well as people who we are less comfortable talking with. It's important to separate the two because we really want to be able to practice our speaking skills with the people who make us feel the most safe. Mutos will try first:

People Mutos feels the most safe speaking with:

Grandpa, Mom, Dad, Sister, and my best friend, Tandy

Now you try...

People you feel the most safe speaking with:

Great job! Now we need to know the people you are the least comfortable speaking with and Mutos will go first:

Teacher, Grackles

Now you try...

People you feel the least comfortable speaking with:

Since Mutos is most comfortable talking to her parents but only speaks to them in a whisper now, we want her to try to speak just a teensy bit louder.

Do you know the difference between a whisper and a shout? I sure hope you do! But sometimes when we are upset, it is hard to speak up. The first thing Mama Gumbo suggests is for Mutos to try to speak with her family again and asks the family to work on encouraging Mutos to speak just a *teensy* bit louder. We can choose a way to remind her to speak up—nothing too obvious. It could be a simple nod of the head. We want her to try to speak up and then once she is doing this without our prodding, we will stop reminding her.

Mutos has been using progressive muscle relaxation to help her feel calmer and things are getting better! Our next step is to find out the bad things Mutos is expecting will happen. Sometimes we expect *really* bad things that will probably never happen, but we still think about them and it makes us unhappy. Let's take a look at Mutos's predictions, and then you can try.

THE PREDICAMENT OF PREDICTING

Did you know that when we make negative predictions about what will happen next, we tend to feel even worse? And it doesn't even matter if the predictions are realistic or not! Let's take a look at some negative predictions we are making.

Write down *exactly* what you are predicting will happen:

I worry I will never be able to speak again because I hurt the grackles. I don't deserve to have friends.

Let's figure out how likely you feel it is that this prediction will come true. We will use this scale:

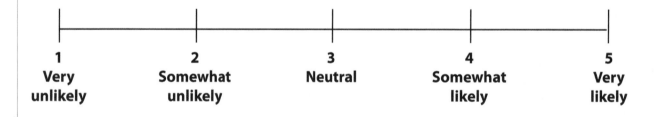

1	2	3	4	5
Very unlikely	**Somewhat unlikely**	**Neutral**	**Somewhat likely**	**Very likely**

What number did you get?

4

Do you have any actual evidence for what you are predicting? If so, what is it?

I haven't been able to speak since they cursed me... but I can whisper now.

Do you have any evidence *against* what you are predicting? If so, list it here:

I don't know anyone else who is under a silence spell, and Mama Gumbo says I will get better, but I just don't know.

Are your predictions based on feelings or logic? For example, if you think something will happen because you feel worried, you are making your predictions based on your feelings. Do you think this is a good way to make decisions?

I feel like I deserve to lose my voice because of what happened to the grackles. They trusted me and I led Ember right to them!

What would you tell a friend who had the same prediction that you do? How would you help him or her?

I would tell her that it was a mistake and that if the grackles understood what happened, they would forgive her.

Finally, how do you think you will feel about the situation you are worried about in a week, a month, or a year? You can write your answer or draw a picture of it here.

I hope I will get my voice back eventually... I wish I could be friends with the grackles. Maybe after a year they might forgive me?

THE PREDICAMENT OF PREDICTING

Now you try it! Did you know that when we make negative predictions about what will happen next, we tend to feel even worse? And it doesn't even matter if the predictions are realistic or not! Let's take a look at some negative predictions we are making.

Write down *exactly* what you are predicting will happen:

Let's figure out how likely you feel it is that this prediction will come true. We will use this scale:

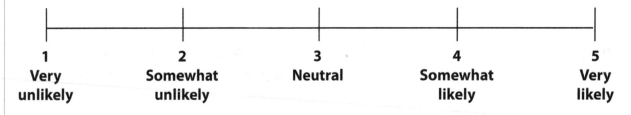

1	2	3	4	5
Very unlikely	**Somewhat unlikely**	**Neutral**	**Somewhat likely**	**Very likely**

What number did you get?

Do you have any actual evidence for what you are predicting? If so, what is it?

Do you have any evidence *against* what you are predicting? If so, list it here:

Are your predictions based on feelings or logic? For example, if you think something will happen because you feel worried, you are making your predictions based on your feelings. Do you think this is a good way to make decisions?

What would you tell a friend who had the same prediction that you do? How would you help him or her?

Finally, how do you think you will feel about the situation you are worried about in a week, a month or a year? You can write your answer or draw a picture of it here.

We are going to try to focus Mutos on more positive things. We want her to tell us what she would like to happen if the very best possible outcome could occur. It's really important to think about what you want to happen, because the more we think about positive things, the more likely they are to occur. Mutos will try and then you can!

POSITIVE PREDICTIONS

The best way to make good things happen is to think positively! Imagine that the problem you are experiencing could be resolved in the absolute best manner possible. Write down your positive prediction here:

The grackles will realize this was all a mistake and apologize to me. They will break the spell and we will all be friends again! I will sing for them all the time.

What would it mean to you if your prediction came true? How would you feel? Write this down or draw a picture of you after the positive prediction comes true!

■ 155

POSITIVE PREDICTIONS

The best way to make good things happen is to think positively! Imagine that the problem you are experiencing could be resolved in the absolute best manner possible. Write down your positive prediction here:

What would it mean to you if your prediction came true? How would you feel? Write this down or draw a picture of you after the positive prediction comes true!

THE THREE Rs:
RELAX, REHEARSE, REDO!

When we are trying to get past our worries, we need to really see ourselves doing well. The best way to do that is to use the three Rs!

Relax! What are the things you do to relax? Write them down here and when you will be using them.

Rehearse! It's important to rehearse the behavior you want to see. How would you like to do that? You can do it alone, in front of a mirror, or with people you trust. Write down your rehearsal plan here:

Redo! A great performance deserves an encore! The next step is to try, try, try again! Give yourself a round of applause for doing so well!

Mutos is getting a lot better: She can speak a little sometimes, but it is still hard for her. She told Mama Gumbo she *really* misses the grackles.

"What stops you from seeing them?" Mama Gumbo asked.

"I think they will yell at me and make me leave. They never want to see me again," Mutos said sadly.

"How do you know?" asked Mama Gumbo. "Did they tell you that?"

Mutos admitted she did not know.

"Then how do you know? Better to find out for yourself than to waste your time worrying about things that aren't happening. I would be happy to go with you."

Mutos was worried, but agreed to try.

As Mama Gumbo and Mutos approached the cave, they noticed it was very quiet. Usually, it was full of laughter and happy singing. And where it used to be glowing with the shine of the grackles' gems, it was strangely dark and dull. What was happening?

Seeing her friends so sad made Mutos cry! She couldn't bear to see them like that. She had to cheer them up, and she knew exactly how to do it. She took a deep breath and let out the most beautiful note ever! Soon she was singing full force, full of love for the grackles.

The grackles heard their friend and were drawn to the amazing sound. They started to smile and sway to the music and instantly their glimmer started to glow! It grew and grew, then surrounded Mutos. The spell was broken!

Mutos embraced her friends and explained she had never intended for Ember to steal from the grackles but that she had been tricked into helping him. The grackles felt ashamed they had behaved with such haste. They couldn't apologize enough.

Mama Gumbo was overjoyed to see them all so happy. "Everyone makes mistakes," she told them all. "We have to talk to each other to make things better. Friends are too important to let one fight ruin the entire relationship."

The grackles and Mutos agreed. Then they all sat down for a nice, long talk!

HELPER SECTION

Selective Mutism

Selective mutism is a curious disorder: No one is clear as to what causes it or why it affects some people and not others. Although it presents with similar symptoms to social anxiety disorder, it differs specifically in the loss of speech. According to the *DSM-5®*, selective mutism consists of the following symptoms:

1. Consistent failure to speak in specific social situations in which there is an expectation for speaking (e.g., at school) despite speaking in other situations.
2. The disturbance interferes with educational or occupational achievement or with social communication.
3. The duration of the disturbance is at least one month (not limited to the first month of school).
4. The failure to speak is not attributable to a lack of knowledge of, or comfort with, the spoken language required in the social situation.
5. The disturbance is not better explained by a communication disorder (e.g., childhood-onset fluency disorder) and does not occur exclusively during the course of autism spectrum disorder, schizophrenia, or another psychotic disorder.

One of the important changes in this diagnosis from the previous designation of selective mutism is that the new criteria express the lack of speech is not willful and instead is a response to anxiety. This is really important, as it changes the focus of treatment completely.

When working with children who have selective mutism, it is important that you focus initially on making the child feel safe and comfortable in the therapeutic setting. If you haven't already, please consult Chapter 4 for more on this.

Sample Selective Mutism Treatment Plan

Goal: Mutos will be able to speak to others regardless of the environment she is in.

Objective One: Mutos will learn three new relaxation techniques to help her calm herself and decrease feelings of anxiety. Mutos agrees to practice these skills at least daily to aid in mastery of these skills.

Objective Two: Mutos will create a plan to begin speaking with others using the "Three Rs" approach. Mutos will come up with a list of safety contacts as well as contacts she would like to begin communicating with.

Objective Three: Mutos will work with her safety contacts to begin in-vivo exposure to improving her communication skills. She will work in session through in-vivo exposure to learn a stimulus-fade method to increase her chances of improving her overall ability to speak at a baseline level with others.

Because children with selective mutism tend to be more difficult to engage, most of your therapeutic tools are in the previous children's section. You will want to work on lots of imaginative play to help them work on their speaking skills.

To help illustrate this point, let's review a case study.

Case Study: Nathan

Nathan is a five-year-old boy presenting for treatment due to selective mutism. Nathan is in kindergarten. Although he started kindergarten interacting regularly with his teacher and classmates, the school year is now halfway through and Nathan does not speak in a regular tone to his teacher. Instead, he tends to whisper or speak unintelligibly.

Nathan is understandably quiet in treatment and we engage in cooperative play for four sessions before he starts to speak to me at all. Once he does, we play a game with a puppet who is hard of hearing. When he speaks to the puppet, the puppet responds, "Aye? I can't hear you, sonny! Ya gotta speak up, Granny's a little deaf!" We play this game often until he is able to begin speaking mostly normally in session.

We then focus on Nathan's teacher and how he feels about her. I have him draw pictures of her and I ask him to describe the best parts of being around his teacher as well as the worst parts.

Nathan tells me he really likes his teacher and is worried he will answer her questions incorrectly. He feels like this would make her not like him, and that would make him sad. We work on what a teacher's job is (to help kids learn) and that she actually *needs* kids to get answers wrong or she cannot educate them. If she can't do her job, she would be very sad, indeed!

We then engage in imaginative play wherein I play the teacher and he is a student who won't speak up, then we switch roles. This is our in-vivo exposure. We talk about what helps the student to speak up and what doesn't. We then work on a stimulus-fade model to remind him to speak up in session. For this, I rely on a simple hand gesture: The teacher will raise her hand slightly, palm up, to indicate "speak up" or "raise the volume." The teacher will also thank him, regardless of his response in order to give him a positive reward for trying.

I will then meet with the teacher and review this stimuli and address how she can respond to students who cannot hear Nathan. I want her to have his back, so I ask that she either tell the kids his answer was great and they have to move on, or change the subject. Once Nathan is speaking up, the teacher only nods her head, and then the stimuli is gone completely.

For the record, Nathan started talking more and his attitude toward school improved. Now they are complaining that he talks *too much* in class! *Sigh* Some people are just never happy.

Chapter 12

WOE, THE DISTRESSED DRAGON

Do you like movies? Woe sure does! In fact, he hopes to one day direct his own movies. One of his first memories as a youngling was going to the movie theatre with his dad to watch his favorite hero, Lone Star Smith, as he took on his enemies armed with nothing more than his trusty fedora and a grappling hook!

Woe was mesmerized by the big screen. The explosions! The bad guys! The showdowns at sundown! There was no end to the excitement he could find whenever he purchased that magical ticket to a world of imagination and drama.

Woe

"Action!" yelled Woe.

"Umm, Woe, I forget... where am I supposed to make my entrance?" asked Hellum.

"Cut!"

Woe shook his head in frustration. "Guys, we talked about this! You're the handsome and suave adventurer, Lone Star Smith, and you are breaking into the hideout of the shifty McCracken brothers to try to save the mayor and get the gold back to the townspeople. Now fix that moustache!"

Woe's friends loved helping him make his vision come to life, working on elaborate sets and costumes. Once they even trekked to the top of the Cliffs of Tiamet for the second installment in his "Zaslo: The Revenge of an Angry Platypus" series.

One bright Saturday morning his best friend, Brewster, ran to his house with great news.

"Woe, guess what? The town is doing a film festival and they are looking for new filmmakers to showcase their work! This could be your big break!"

Woe couldn't believe his luck! He assembled his crew and they were all full of excitement. They were going to film "Lone Star: The Blind Oracle," a mind-blowing, special effects-laden, heartwarming tale written and directed entirely by Woe. First prize would be his for sure!

They started working night and day; anytime they weren't in school, the team was together. They even came up with a name for their production team: WHOA!, a delightful take on Woe's name and their combined enthusiasm. The team set forth to tell the compelling story of a team of young, intrepid dragons as they search for treasure and mystery among the bluffs of great Mount Tolkien. Their activities held the townspeople in awe. They would show up to watch them film and were very supportive of Woe's first large-scale

cinematic adventure. The General donated some uniforms and Mama Gumbo offered box lunches to the crew to keep their spirits up.

It was time to film the exciting climax for the film. His lead actors, Zephyr and Brewster, were already in their places. All they had to do was set up the shot.

"Okay, so we have to get this timing perfect," Woe said. "Zephyr, you are going to run down from the cliff with the angry bad guys in hot pursuit. Bad guys numbers 1 through 4, on your mark! Brewster, once they hit their mark, we will do a close shot of you running after them.

Axyl, remember: You are Baron Von Firstenburger. You MUST capture Shannondow and Lone Star before they make it to their rendezvous point with the government and turn over the statue of the blind oracle."

The crew were tired. Axyl adjusted his eye patch and yawned.

"Woe! We're tired and hungry!" said Zephyr. "We can't keep doing this again and again! We need a break."

"Just do it once more," Woe called. "We can get it before nightfall."

"Come on!" Brewster said. "We're hungry and need a break. Let's pick it up in the morning!"

The crew agreed and started packing up their things. Soon Woe was left all alone.

Later that night, Woe was in his room working on editing the day's film. Certain parts just weren't working together. The big build up to the final chase? You could see where the crew had pushed rocks to make it look like a landslide. And was Axyl wearing a watch?! This was supposed to be a vintage piece!

Woe laid his head down on his desk. His work would never be done! *Oh, man!* he thought. *How will I finish in time for the festival if my actors and crew can't get it?*

Just then he heard a slight tapping at his window. Intrigued, he went to investigate.

"Hey, kid," said a strange voice. "Heard you were competing in the film thing. I am a... concerned citizen, and I want to make sure you show them your best work. I got a little present for you."

Do you recognize that dragon? It's Ember! Bet he's up to no good.

Confused, Woe stammered, "That's quite all right, I couldn't possibly accept something from a stranger—"

But Woe stopped in his tracks when he saw what the stranger had placed on his desk—a brand new camera.

"She's a beaut, ain't she?" the stranger continued. "This is an XP900, top of the line. Gets you the best shots possible. I want you to have it."

"Umm, no, I—" began Woe.

"Please, I insist! I am an avid film lover, and I really want to see what a *real* director can do with such an amazing piece of equipment. Take a closer look!"

Woe examined the camera. He had never seen such a great piece of equipment. But he couldn't keep it... could he?

"Well, thanks, mister, but—" Woe was shocked to see that the stranger was completely gone. He closed the window and looked at the camera.

Well, I don't want to be rude, Woe thought.

The next morning the crew was ready to go. They seemed to be in a much better mood than the night before.

"Hey, Woe!" said Axyl. "How was your night?"

Woe explained the strange meeting he had and showed his friends the camera. They all agreed that it seemed quite extraordinary.

"Show us how it works!" Zephyr implored him.

"Okay," said Woe. "Let's shoot some film!"

Everyone took their places to film last night's exciting climax. Bad guys were in place, good guys were at the mark. The crew was on standby to reenact the rockslide. Everyone was really excited.

The action was seamless! Shannondow ran gracefully away from the McCrackens while Lone Star was in hot pursuit. At the last second, Baron Von Firstenburger jumped in front of Lone Star, only to be taken down by his trusty grappling hook and a resulting rockslide. It was better than Woe had ever envisioned.

"Cut! Great job, everyone!" Cheers were heard from all around! Even the townspeople who had gathered to watch were impressed.

"Let's watch it!" Brewster suggested, grabbing a lunch from Mama Gumbo.

"Okay, let me rewind the tape and we can watch. You guys are going to be so proud! It's our best work yet!" Woe hit the rewind button and was shocked to see his *friends* rewinding! Like magic, Axyl, Zephyr, and the rest of the cast did everything they just did, backward.

"The camera is rewinding them!" Woe gasped.

"Stop the tape, Woe!" implored his boom mic operator, Elyot.

As soon as he did, Zephyr and Axyl started the scene exactly as they had again. But as soon as they got to the end, the camera rewound itself and they started yet again!

"Oh my goodness! It's like they are in a trance! They just keep acting out this scene, over and over again," props master Kither said.

"What have I done?" Woe gasped.

Mama Gumbo had heard the commotion and called out to the intrepid film team.

"What on earth is going on?" she asked

"They're—they're trapped!" Woe gestured toward his friends, who seemed to be stuck in some type of time warp. They would begin the scene, get to a certain place, then move backwards in time and do it again in exactly the same way.

"How did this happen?" asked Mama Gumbo.

Woe showed her the camera and explained the strange meeting from the night before. Mama Gumbo took a closer look at the camera, then took a small cloth out to wipe it.

"Ah-ha!" she exclaimed. "It is just as I thought. See this strange shimmer?" Sure enough, there was an odd, smoky purple color on the cloth. "Take a sniff," she offered.

"Ugh! It smells like pepper!" said Woe, holding his nose.

"Mmm-hmm," replied Mama Gumbo. "That's Ember. The person you spoke with, was he wearing a beanie hat?"

"Yes..."

"Oh, that Ember! Always causing so much trouble. I should have known he would try to sabotage the film festival after he wasn't picked. This camera is enchanted. Whatever it records becomes trapped inside, forced to obey the controls on the camera. Press pause for a moment."

Woe did so, and Zephyr and Axyl suddenly stood as still as statues.

"Now, speed it up," she suggested.

Zephyr and Brewster started moving at an accelerated pace, talking quickly and racing through their scene.

"What do we do?" asked Woe. "This is all my fault! If I hadn't asked them to work so hard, or been so focused on winning the festival..." He started to cry.

"Woe, don't be so hard on yourself," said Mama Gumbo. "Ember knew what he was doing when he gave you this. But I know a bit about magical things as well, and any spell that can be cast can be broken. This spell gets more powerful the more you blame yourself. It is a guilt spell. It only works when something bad happens and you blame yourself. So the guilt spell forces you to see the bad thing happen again and again in the hopes of fixing it this time. But it can't be fixed, you see: What is done is done. Instead, you have to accept what happened and then *learn* from it. What was it that happened right before you saw Ember yesterday?"

Woe thought hard. "We were filming and I wasn't being very patient." Woe felt ashamed of himself, but continued. "I really wanted to get through the chase scene before nightfall, but everyone was being silly. I yelled at them and told them to stop messing around. I wished they would just do what I said so we could finish the project."

Mama Gumbo put a comforting arm around Woe. "If you could do it again, what would you do?"

"I guess I would think that maybe they were being silly because they needed a break. Maybe I would listen to their feedback a little bit more and not be so tough on them. Maybe then Ember wouldn't have tricked me into trapping my friends."

He watched as his friends kept running through an unending loop of action, continually doing the same things over and over. Woe felt so upset this had happened. It was all his fault!

"I just wanted so badly to get this done right and win the festival! But what good is winning without your friends?"

Suddenly, something amazing happened! Woe's enchanted camera began to gurgle and smoke. It started to shake and sputter. Then it began to glow brighter and brighter until it suddenly vanished!

"Woe? Woe, what is going on?" asked Zephyr. She was blinking her eyes.

All of his friends were back to normal! Woe ran to his friends in relief.

"Everyone, I am so sorry I let my need to make the perfect movie get in the way of our friendship. I understand if you all want to quit," Woe said.

"No way!" exclaimed Brewster. "We are all behind you, Woe! Let's get this thing done!"

Everyone whooped and hollered. They were all so excited.

"Remember what you learned," Mama Gumbo said as she left.

Woe set out to finish his movie, but this time he tried to listen more to his friends. He made sure that they were having fun when they worked, not just getting the job done. And at the film festival, he was overjoyed to receive a first place trophy in the "up and coming category" to share with his friends!

Have you ever had something happen to you and you felt like it just kept replaying again and again in your head? Woe's enchanted camera did just that—it kept showing him the same things over and over again, and reminding him of how upset he was.

Sometimes something bad happens to us and it replays in our heads just like we have a magical movie camera showing us the same things over and over again. We feel really bad about what happened, and it makes us feel mad or sad. We may blame ourselves for things that are completely outside of our control. Sometimes we find ourselves having nightmares or trouble eating.

So how do we help ourselves feel better? The first step is taking good care of yourself! That means resuming your regular daily activities, like going to school, spending time with family, and eating and sleeping normally. This would be a great time to revisit the "Things I Like to Do" worksheet in Chapter 2.

The next step will be to work on your stress levels. One of the best ways to help your body relax is to take deep, healthy breaths. Woe likes blowing bubbles to help him to deep breathe because he has to take in a really deep breath and then let it out in a slow and controlled way. Three of those breaths and he feels calmer instantly.

It's important to take good care of yourself and focus on being positive in the moment. Keep at it and you will start to feel better!

Post-traumatic stress (PTSD)

Post-traumatic stress disorder (PTSD) can impact anyone at any time. It is triggered by exposure to an upsetting event and leads to startled responses, severe anxiety, and an overall feeling of fear even when the person is not in any actual danger. It is important to note that people respond to upsetting events differently, even when they all witness the exact same event together. This phenomenon is known as the Rashomon effect after the 1950 film *Rashomon* by Akira Kurosawa. In the film, four people witness a murder and give contradictory accounts of what happened.

The Rashomon effect means each individual has their own individual response to trauma and treatment will be tailored to the individual's needs.

One of the first things you will need to do is make certain the child is not experiencing opportunistic emotional disturbances. This means evaluating the child for depression as well as addressing any anger that may be lingering. Some children will hold onto anger as they feel this keeps them connected to the loss. I have had children tell me that if they let go of the anger they will feel as if they betrayed the person or thing they have lost due to the trauma.

I firmly believe anger needs to have its moment: We need to find a way to let it out in a positive, controlled manner. Some kids like to yell their anger, some like to hit things (safe things, like a punching bag or a pillow), and others engage in symbolic destruction, such as ripping up a picture or tearing up a letter. Work with the child to find out how they would like to try to address their anger. This may take some trial and error, as many children do not know how to express anger appropriately.

Sample PTSD Treatment Plan

Goal: Work on describing the history and nature of PTSD symptoms. When able to do so safely, describe the traumatic event in as much detail as possible. Verbalize any symptoms of depression, including any suicidal ideation.

Objective One: If needed, cooperate with an evaluation by a physician for medication management. Participate in individual and/or group therapy sessions focused on PTSD. Learn about how PTSD develops and be able to list the common symptoms of PTSD.

Objective Two: Engage in play therapy to help tell the story of the trauma. Learn calming and coping strategies in session to help manage challenging situations related to trauma. Identify, challenge, and replace fearful self-talk with reality-based, positive self-talk.

Objective Three: Participate in imaginal and in-vivo exposure to trauma-related memories to aid with maladaptive thoughts and behaviors. Learn and implement thought-stopping to manage intrusive, unwanted thoughts. Work on creating hopeful and positive goals regarding the future.

Remind children that although it is normal to avoid things linked to the trauma, the longer they avoid such things the more firmly rooted the trauma becomes and the harder it is to move forward. It is important to encourage them to resume their daily activities and to return to the location of the trauma, if appropriate, once they are feeling safer.

When you engage in trauma treatment with children for PTSD, play therapy is your friend! The only rule is to avoid reenacting the event. Don't worry: Many children will do so themselves when they play. You will need to dust off your primer for Freudian psychology and work on interpreting their play.

The number one thing about working with traumatized children is helping them to feel safe and secure. If they feel comforted by the people in their lives, they tend to get better. Be patient! It is hard to get over painful things. If you can provide lots of encouragement and positive affirmations, the child will begin to improve. Remember that the goal of treatment is mastering the trauma, meaning that the child feels he or she learned something from the event. Sometimes the only thing we learn is our great capacity to love and to recover from a terrible situation in order to grow and move forward in our lives.

RERUN, THE REPETITIVE DRAGON

See this picture? This is Rerun and her Nana (that's what we call our grandmas around here).

Don't they look so happy? Rerun absolutely adores her grandmother, and she tries to spend as much time as possible with her. They like watching movies together and going for walks. But most of all, Rerun really loves knowing her Nana is around and will be there for her whenever she needs her.

Nana gave Rerun a big scare last winter, though. There had been a big snow storm and Rerun was planning to come over to help her with shoveling some snow (with Nana's famous hot chocolate as her reward!). Unfortunately, Rerun overslept and was still sleeping when Rerun's mom received a phone call that Nana had fallen in the snow.

Rerun and her family rushed to the hospital. Would Nana be okay? The whole ride there, Rerun kept blaming herself. If only she hadn't overslept, Nana would not have been out shoveling alone and she would not have been hurt.

I'm so selfish! she chided herself. *How hard is it to get your lazy butt out of bed? Because you couldn't be bothered to wake up on time, Nana got hurt! How could you be so awful?*

The hospital was cold and smelled like bleach. It was so noisy and scary. Rerun huddled next to her parents and brothers, scared of what they might find. A kind nurse helped them find Nana's room.

Rerun

"Nana!" Rerun ran to her grandmother's side.

"Well, I've made a mess of myself today," Nana said, gesturing at her leg, which was bound in a bright white cast and suspended from the ceiling.

"What did they do to you?" Rerun asked through her tears.

"Oh, silly, it's what I did to myself. I went out to shovel like a silly billy, and before you know it, I went splat! I fell right on my back. Knocked the wind clear out of me! Oh, Rerun, I should have waited for you."

But Rerun knew better. It was *she* who had failed. If it weren't for her, Nana would be fine right now. She was so ashamed, she could barely even look Nana in the eye. She decided she would wear her snow boots all the time to help keep Nana safe, and every time she visited Nana in the hospital she would hop on one leg three times before she entered the main doors and do the same thing when she left. She felt like doing this would keep all the bad illnesses in the hospital from following her home.

After a few days, Nana was out of the hospital. Rerun *knew* it was because of the hopping! She knew she would have to keep doing it in order to keep Nana safe. Rerun swore that she would never let this type of thing happen to Nana ever again. She went through Nana's house top to bottom to remove anything that might hurt her.

"Rerun, what are you doing?" asked Nana. "Those are my knitting needles!"

Rerun decided that anytime snow was in the forecast, she would sleep over at Nana's the night before so she could help her. And she insisted that Nana call her before she left the house, when she arrived at her destination, and when she was back home. If Nana didn't call, Rerun would call her incessantly until she answered. Sometimes she would cry until Nana answered the phone. Once Nana answered, Rerun would hop up and down three times to make sure that Nana stayed safe.

Initially, Nana thought it was sweet that her little grandchild was so interested in helping her. But after a bit of time, it got tiresome. Rerun was constantly monitoring Nana, checking on her all the time to make sure she was safe. She would cut up Nana's food for her and watch her eat, afraid she might choke. Whenever the forecast called for snow, Rerun felt like she was on edge. She would start to pick at her nails and sometimes they would bleed. She would think about that morning, *that awful morning,* when she woke up to hear how her grandmother had been hurt. Then she would remember the long ride to the hospital and the smell of the bleach as they tried to find Nana in a maze of gurneys and nurses, everything beeping and ringing while the lights buzzed angrily.

Brrr! Rerun didn't want to say anything, but she had started to have nightmares about their time in the hospital. Even worse, she would dream that the whole day was happening all over again but this time Nana was injured even worse. Each time Rerun was reminded it was completely and utterly her fault Nana had been hurt.

Soon Rerun was picking at her nails even more. She was terrified about going back to the hospital so she started to be very careful about germs. *They were everywhere!* She was constantly washing her hands, countertops, and anything else she could get her hands on. She started to worry more and more about Nana. Sometimes when Rerun was talking with others they complained that she would "blank out" and not pay attention. In fact, Rerun was lost in thought, thinking about how to protect her family from getting sick.

The time had finally come for Nana to have her cast taken off. She had noticed Rerun had been very preoccupied with germs and thought having Rerun accompany her to the hospital might help her.

"I can't," said Rerun. The thought of going to the hospital, being surrounded by all of those germs! It was too much to bear! She started to cry.

Rerun told her Nana how it was her fault that Nana had been injured, and that if she had not been so lazy Nana would have never gotten hurt.

"Rerun, that isn't true! The only person who broke my fool leg was me. Even if you had been there, I still might have gotten hurt."

"But I could have stopped you!" Rerun said.

"You don't know that!" Nana said, hugging her close. "In fact, I'm glad you weren't there. I have nightmares I might have hurt myself while you were here, and then you would have had to see that."

"*You* have nightmares?" Rerun asked.

"Oh, yes," Nana assured her. "I have nightmares you might have seen me get hurt. I am so grateful it happened when you weren't around."

"But I wish I had been! Isn't that funny—you are grateful for the thing I am angry about!" Rerun chuckled.

"All of life is a matter of perception, child. I see my leg breaking that morning as a blessing and you see it as a curse. I guess that's because we love each other so much. But we can't go back and change it and I'm much better know. What do we need to do to let this go? And don't think I haven't noticed the hopping and the picking."

Rerun hung her head in shame. "I know I'm weird! I don't know what's wrong with me. It doesn't make any sense, the things I am doing. But I feel like I have to do it or something else bad will happen."

"I know something you can do that will absolutely help *me* out. You can come with me to remove my cast, and while we are there we can ask Dr. Prudens about how you are feeling. Sometimes talking to someone *outside* of the problem will help. What do you think? I could really use your help."

Rerun decided that maybe helping Nana remove her cast would help her feel better about the situation. Nana explained she would never blame Rerun for what happened to her leg and even listed ways it had helped her.

"For example," Nana began, "I don't have to take the garbage out!" They both laughed. "Rerun, you can't control the world, you can only react to it. The strongest of us learns that we have to grow with change."

Rerun helped the doctors remove the cast and even got to help Nana take her very first step without it. She was so proud!

What do you think about Rerun? She loves her Nana so much she is acting strangely to try to protect her. Sometimes our minds play tricks on us: They tell us to do things that can't possibly affect the outcome of a situation and then make us feel like if we don't do these things, bad things will happen.

Do you remember some of the strange things Rerun was doing? She was picking at her nails, hopping up and down three times, cleaning constantly, and calling her grandmother all of the time.

She even slept over at her grandmother's to keep an eye on her, and she wore her snow boots constantly. Have you ever done something unusual and then felt like you had to do it a certain number of times or in a certain order? This is what we call a compulsion.

Don't be afraid! Compulsions don't have to control your life. Rerun met with Dr. Prudens, who explained it was very normal to feel upset and try to find ways to stop bad things from happening. He worked with her to be more mindful of her behaviors and start reducing them, first in terms of how often she did them and then in regard to doing them at all.

After some time, Rerun was feeling much, much better! You can meet with special doctors to help you, too! They will help you relax and

then work on getting rid of the compulsions that are upsetting you. By working together, we can all get better!

Obsessive-Compulsive Disorder (OCD)

Obsessive-compulsive disorder (OCD) is defined by the *DSM-5®* as a condition in which an individual experiences intrusive thoughts, images, or impulses, which create a high degree of emotional distress and often lead to feelings of guilt or disgust. It can sometimes involve irrational beliefs, meaning it is irrational to think that hopping up and down three times will keep someone safe, but a person with OCD will believe this to be true and continue to engage in the behavior.

There tends to be a genetic pattern in OCD, although scientists have yet to be able to discover which genes are specifically involved. However, if a person has a first degree relative with OCD, they have a higher probability of being diagnosed with the disorder.

There are six basic categories for OCD obsession/compulsions:

1. **Checking disorders:** The need to check on things for safety such as checking locks, flipping light switches, checking a wallet or a document repeatedly
2. **Contamination:** Preoccupation with germs and keeping healthy
3. **Fear of losing control:** Concerns about acting out aggressively, yelling obscenities, stealing things, having violent images in one's mind
4. **Fear of harm:** Preoccupation with being held against one's will or being wrongly accused
5. **Symmetry and orderliness:** An obsessive need to have a certain number of something, needing things to have a specific order or direction
6. **Intrusive thoughts:** Experiencing upsetting and ongoing thoughts about relationships (e.g., someone thinking they are married to a celebrity they have never met); magical thinking (e.g., believing you can jump up and down in an elevator and it won't crash); sexual thoughts (e.g., fear of being raped or raping someone else with no history or reason to believe this will occur); religious thoughts (e.g., praying incessantly or becoming involved in religious rituals that are outside of what the religion typically endorses); and violent thoughts (e.g., seeing oneself engaging in acts of extreme violence)

In true OCD, the compulsions may jump from one category to another. So the child may start out with a contamination issue but once this resolves they develop a fear of harm. When you work on OCD with children, you will need to address the underlying anxiety as well as the current obsessions and/or compulsions.

Sample OCD Treatment Plan

Goal: Significantly reduce time involved with or interference from obsessions. Significantly reduce frequency of compulsive or ritualistic behaviors. Improve daily functioning to a consistent level with minimal interference from obsessions and compulsions.

Objective One: Describe the nature, history, and severity of obsessive thoughts and/or compulsive behavior. Complete a psychological testing evaluation, if necessary, to assess the nature and severity of the obsessive-compulsive problem. If needed, cooperate with an evaluation by a physician for psychotropic medication. Learn and verbalize an understanding of the rationale for treatment of OCD.

Objective Two: Identify and replace biased, fearful self-talk and beliefs. Work with therapist to participate in repeated imaginal exposure to feared external and/or internal triggers that tend to lead to compulsions. Complete homework assignments involving in-vivo exposure to feared external and/or internal cues.

Objective Three: Learn thought-stopping techniques to reduce the frequency of obsessive thoughts. Work on learning mindfulness skills to separate the trigger from the compulsion. Be able to gauge the level of stress on a stress scale to reinforce positive stress-coping skills. Identify supportive people and resources and how to access these when feeling more stressed.

Feel free to utilize any of the general anxiety treatments in Chapter 5 to begin working on anxiety symptoms so that the child can begin to feel less worried. Once that happens, the child will be introduced to understanding the relationship between the compulsion, the stressor, and the anxiety level. I always let kids know that when their compulsions increase, it tells them that there is something upsetting in their environment, either physically or emotionally. I ask children, *do you engage in the compulsion because you want to or because the OCD wants you to?* This is important because once the child recognizes that the compulsion does not help with the overall anxiety, it is easier to break that cycle.

The next step will then be to reduce the response frequency. That means we will practice being exposed to the stressor and changing the response. So if the child typically quickly clicks the light switch off and on five times, we will first try to switch it off slowly. Then we will try to do it only four times, then three, and so on. If the child isn't ready for that, you will instead put more time in between the clicks. Take care not to tell them to wait a certain amount, as the child may then obsess about that number.

Finally, if the child isn't responding to treatment or has begun engaging in increasingly dangerous behaviors, a referral for medication evaluation may be necessary. But please know that I treat many people for OCD who do not require medication, but they do need ongoing treatment and increasing mindfulness of what their stress triggers are so that they can maintain optimal functioning.

Chapter 14

EMBER, THE FINAL DRAGON

HELPER SECTION

Did you notice Ember, sneaking around throughout our book? He is always trying to cause some trouble! Here are some quick tips for when you have your own little Ember in your life, and you're having some trouble helping your little dragon to feel better.

Ember

For help with perseverative thoughts:

1. Try some pink elephants (again!)

Remember this little gem from Chapter 5? Try it again, but with some extra umph! Thoughts are linear, so in order to stop a thought, you need to stop the linear progression of a thought. Your brain cannot perceive self-negatives, so we can trick it into stopping a thought by telling it *not* to do something. Usually, I use the term "pink elephants" to help. I tell the child to say the thought they are perseverating on out loud, and I let them know that

saying it out loud doesn't give it any power: It can't make it happen or make it stop happening. Thoughts are *not* actions. I let kids know they can think the thought as much as they want and as often as they want as long as they *do not* think about pink elephants. You then reiterate this: DO NOT THINK ABOUT PINK ELEPHANTS! Keep saying it until the child starts to giggle a bit. If it works, the thought they are having will be stopped in its tracks and replaced by giant pink elephants! They can practice this whenever they wish, and the more they practice, the more control they will have over their thoughts. Easy peasy!

2. Try temperature control

Thought stopping works best when it introduces a real danger to combat the fake danger. This is why dangerous thought-stopping techniques such as hair-pulling (which can become trichotillomania), skin picking (which can become excoriation) and self-mutilation (such as cutting behaviors) are so addictive to kids with anxiety; they stop the scary thoughts quickly but have to be revisited to keep those thoughts at bay. Try changing temperature, especially in the palms of the hand, to help with extreme anxiety. You can do this by having the child place something cold in their hand, such as ice (clearly do *not* apply this technique to children who are ice burners) or use cold stones (you can freeze them beforehand or use the decorative stones found in hobby stores. The ones used for decoration are plastic and typically are naturally cold to the touch. You can also use things in the environment: a cold drink, snow, cold water.

For anyone who has attended my trainings, I often review a method I use to help children who engage in cutting behaviors. This method is only to be used with kids who are old enough to maintain personal safety and who are cutting superficially with no history of suicidal tendencies.

As you know, I like to play with the brain, so when I am trying to outsmart a cutting urge, I want to trick the brain into thinking it is self-harming, as the process of self-harm is what stops the thought. We are going to use a method I call "**The Icy Orange**." When you introduce a child to this, you let them know they will need to purchase an orange and then freeze it in the place where they most typically cut (e.g., their home). I let kids know that the next time they want to cut, or if they have already cut superficially and have an additional urge to do so but know they need to stop, they must first go get this frozen orange. Their task is to get the orange, peel it, eat it, and then see if they still want to

cut. It is important you don't explain how it works until the child has found it to be effective a few times (you don't want to ruin the magic!).

I tried this with a 14-year-old and at her next session she appeared with an orange, which she quickly threw at my head! When I asked her what was wrong, she told me my "weird orange thing" had messed her up. She told me she didn't cut herself and what was worse, she had trouble focusing on what she had been upset about before she tried to peel the orange. Here's how it works:

1. When you freeze an orange, it gets *extremely* cold. When you put it in your hands to peel it, you expose the nerve endings in your hands to this cold, and the nerves focus in on this. Cold is a real danger! This forces all of the attention toward the *real* danger and away from the imaginary danger.

2. When the child tries to peel this orange, the hands get even colder. The act of peeling an orange is very similar to self-mutilation: You dig into it with your nails and tear it open, just like one might tear into their own flesh. This allows the brain to visually see the impact of self-mutilation.

3. Once the nails have punctured the orange's skin, you will get pith (that's the weird yellow bit under the skin) under your nails, and this *looks* like your own skin. It feels similar, as well. Your brain now has experienced the same visceral experience of self-mutilation, with the cold of the orange substituting for the pain of cutting.

4. Finally, if the child ends up eating the orange, they place the ice-cold bits into their mouth, chew them and swallow them. This transports very cold items into the body, again focusing the body on the *real* dangers of freezing and stopping any other thoughts.

References

For your convenience, purchasers can download and print
worksheets and handouts from www.pesi.com/Dragons

Abela, J. R. (2006). Phobic and anxiety disorders in children and adolescents: A clinician's guide to effective psychosocial and pharmacological interventions. *Journal of Cognitive Psychotherapy, 20*(1), 109.

Aldridge, K. (1993). The use of music to relieve pre-operational anxiety in children attending day surgery. *Australian Journal of Music Therapy, 4,* 19+. Retrieved from http://www.questia.com

Altman, C., Sommer, J. L., & McGoey, K. E. (2009). Anxiety in early childhood: What do we know? *Journal of Early Childhood and Infant Psychology, 5,* 157+. Retrieved from http://www.questia.com

American Psychiatric Association. (2013). *Diagnostic and statistical manual of mental disorders (5th ed.).* Mar 25, 2017.

Augner, C. (2011). Associations of subjective sleep quality with depression score, anxiety, physical symptoms and sleep onset latency in students. *Central European Journal of Public Health, 19*(2), 115+. Retrieved from http://www.questia.com

Baer, R. A. (2003). Mindfulness training as clinical intervention: A conceptual and empirical review. *Clinical Psychology: Science and Practice, 10,* 125–143.

Bahali, K., Tahiroglu, A. Y., Avci, A., & Seydaoglu, G. (2011). Parental psychological symptoms and familial risk factors of children and adolescents who exhibit school fefusal. *East Asian Archives of Psychiatry, 21*(4), 164+. Retrieved from http://www.questia.com

Barry, C. M., Nelson, L. J., & Christofferson, J. L. (2013). Asocial and afraid: An examination of shyness and anxiety in emerging adulthood. *Journal of Family Studies, 19*(1), 2+. Retrieved from http://www.questia.com

Bishop, S. R., Laue, M., Shapiro, S., Carlson, L., Anderson, N. D., Carmody, J., et al. (2004). Mindfulness: A proposed operational definition. *Clinical Psychology: Science & Practice, 11,* 230–241.

Blashfield, J., & Bosker, G. (1983). *Brainstorm* (pp. 29-24). Portland, OR: Marble Press.

Brown, K. W., & Ryan, R. M. (2003). The benefits of being present: Mindfulness and its role in psychological well-being. *Journal of Personality and Social Psychology, 84,* 822–848.

Burgess, K. B., & Younger, A. J. (2006). Self-schemas, anxiety, somatic and depressive symptoms in socially withdrawn children and adolescents. *Journal of Research in Childhood Education, 20*(3), 175+. Retrieved from http://www.questia.com

Calvete, E., Orue, I., & Hankin, B. L. (2013). Early maladaptive schemas and social anxiety in adolescents: The mediating role of anxious automatic thoughts. *Journal of Anxiety Disorders, 27*(3), 278-288.

Cantz, P., & Castle, M. (2013). A psycho-biblical response to death anxiety: Separation and individuation dynamics in the Babel narrative. *Journal of Psychology and Theology, 41*(4), 327+. Retrieved from http://www.questia.com

Choate-Summers, M. L., Freeman, J. B., Garcia, A. M., Coyne, L., Przeworski, A., & Leonard, H. L. (2008). Clinical considerations when tailoring cognitive behavioral treatment for young children with obsessive compulsive disorder. *Education & Treatment of Children, 31*(3), 395+. Retrieved from http://www.questia.com

Choi, Y. K. (2010). The effect of music and progressive muscle relaxation on anxiety, fatigue, and quality of life in family caregivers of hospice patients. *Journal of Music Therapy, 47*(1), 53+. Retrieved from http://www.questia.com

Christoforou, A., & Kipper, D. A. (2006). The spontaneity assessment inventory (SAI), anxiety, obsessive-compulsive tendency, and temporal orientation. *Journal of Group Psychotherapy, Psychodrama & Sociometry, 59*(1), 23+. Retrieved from http://www.questia.com

Clark, D. M., Salkovskis, P. M., Öst, L. G., Breitholtz, E., Koehler, K. A., Westling, B. E., et al. (1997). Misinterpretation of body sensations in panic disorder. *Journal of Consulting and Clinical Psychology, 65,* 203–213.

Clark, D. M. (1986). A cognitive approach to panic. *Behavior Research and Therapy, 24*(4), 461-470.

Conklin, S. M., Gianaros, P. J., Brown, S. M., Yao, J. K., Haririr, A. R., Manuck, S. B., et. al. (2007). Long-chain omega-3 fatty acid intake is associated positively with corticolimbic gray matter volume in healthy adults. *Neuroscience Letters, 421*(3), 209-212.

Craske, M. G., Rapee, R. M., & Barlow, D. H. (1988). The significance of panic-expectancy for individual patterns of avoidance. *Behavior Therapy, 19,* 577–592.

Cristea, I., Benga, O., & Opre, A. (2006). The comparative efficiency of a rational-emotive educational intervention for anxiety in 3rd grade children: An analysis of relevant developmental constraints. *Cognitie, Creier, Comportament, 10*(4), 637+. Retrieved from http://www.questia. com

DeBecker, Gavin. (1999). *The gift of fear.* New York: Dell Publishers.

De Matos, M. G., Tomé, G., Borges, A. I., Manso, D., Ferreira, P., & Ferreira, A. (2008). Anxiety, depression and coping strategies: Improving the evaluation and the understanding of these dimensions during pre-adolescence and adolescence. *Journal of Evidence-Based Psychotherapies, 8*(2), 169+. Retrieved from http://www.questia.com

Derakshan, N., & Eysenck, M. W. (1997). Interpretative biases for one's own behavior and physiology in high-trait-anxious individuals and repressors. *Journal of Personality and Social Psychology, 73*(4), 816-825.

Deshpande, S., Vidya, G., Bendre, N., & Ghate, M. (2011). Children with medically unexplained pain symptoms: Categorization and effective management. Indian *Journal of Psychological Medicine, 33*(2). Retrieved from http://www.questia.com

Dia, D. A., & Harrington, D. (2006). What about me? Siblings of children with an anxiety disorder. *Social Work Research, 30*(3), 183+. Retrieved from http://www.questia.com

Drewes, A. A., (Ed.). (2009). *Blending play therapy with cognitive behavioral therapy: Evidence-based and other effective treatments and techniques.* Hoboken, NJ. John Wiley & Sons.

Feather, J. S., & Ronan, K. R. (2006). Trauma-focused cognitive behavioural therapy for abused children with posttraumatic stress disorder: A pilot study. New Zealand Journal of Psychology, 35(3), 132+. Retrieved from http://www.questia.com

Ferrara, P., Romani, L., Bottaro, G., Ianniello, F., Fabrizio, G. C., Chiaretti, A., & Alvaro, F. (2013). The physical and mental health of children in foster care. *Iranian Journal of Public Health, 42*(4), 368+. Retrieved from http://www.questia.com

Fralich, T. (2007). *Cultivating lasting happiness: A 7-step guide to mindfulness.* Eau Claire, WI: PESI, LLC.

Geist, E. (2010). The anti-anxiety curriculum: Combating math anxiety in the classroom. *Journal of Instructional Psychology, 37*(1), 24+. Retrieved from http://www.questia.com

Ginsburg, G. S., Becker, K. D., Drazdowski, T. K., & Tein, J. (2012). Treating anxiety disorders in inner city schools: Results from a pilot randomized controlled trial comparing CBT and usual care. *Child & Youth Care Forum, 41*(1), 1-19.

Gosch, E. A., Flannery-Shroeder, E., Mauro, C. F., & Compton, S. N. (2006). Principles of cognitive-behavioral therapy for anxiety disorders in children. *Journal of Cognitive Psychotherapy. 20*(3), 247. Retrieved from http://www.questia.com

Gothelf, D., et al. (2006). Follow-up of preschool children with severe emotional and behavioral symptoms. *The Israel Journal of Psychiatry and Related Sciences, 43*(1), 16+. Retrieved from http://www.questia.com

Graham, A. A., & Coplan, R. J. (2012). Shyness, sibling relationships, and young children's socioemotional adjustment at preschool. *Journal of Research in Childhood Education, 26*(4), 435+. Retrieved from http://www.questia.com

Grant, V. V., Bagnell, A. L., Chambers, C. T., & Stewart, S. H. (2009). Early temperament prospectively predicts anxiety in later childhood. *Canadian Journal of Psychiatry, 54*(5), 320+. Retrieved from http://www.questia.com

Gratz, K. L., Tull, M. T., & Wagner, A. W. (2005). Applying DBT mindfulness skills to the treatment of clients with anxiety disorders. In Orsillo, S. M., & Roemer, L. (Eds.) *Acceptance and mindfulness-based approaches to anxiety: Series in anxiety and related disorders,* 147-161. New York: Springer Science + Business Media, LLC.

Griffiths, K. (2008). The worry busters program: An anxiety intervention for primary aged children. *Health Sociology Review, 17*(1), 113+. Retrieved from http://www.questia.com

Grover, R. L., Hughes, A. A., Bergman, R. L., & Kingery, J. N. (2006). Treatment modifications based on childhood anxiety diagnosis: Demonstrating the flexibility in manualized treatment. *Journal of Cognitive Psychotherapy, 20*(3), 275+. Retrieved from http://www.questia.com

Howard, R. (2008). Movin' on up: Transitioning to kindergarten, with tips for easing anxiety. *Childhood Education, 84*(4), 238. Retrieved from http://www.questia.com

Hyman, B. M., & Pedrick, C. (2010). *The OCD workbook (3rd edition)*. Oakland, CA: New Harbinger Publications, Inc.

Igelman, R., Taylor, N., Gilbert, A., Ryan, B., Steinberg, A., Wilson, C., & Mann, G. (2007). Creating more trauma-informed services for children using assessment-focused tools. *Child Welfare, 86*(5), 15+. Retrieved from http://www.questia.com

Kabat-Zinn, J., Massion, M. D., Kristeller, J. L., Peterson, L. G., Fletcher, K. E., Pbert, L., et al. (1992). Effectiveness of a meditation-based stress reduction program in the treatment of anxiety disorders. *American Journal of Psychiatry, 149,* 936-943.

Kadohisa, M., Rolls, E. T., & Verhagen, J. V. (2005). Neuronal representations of stimuli in the mouth: The primate insular taste cortex, orbitofrontal cortex and amygdala. *Chemical Senses, 40*(4), 401-419.

Kearney, C. A., & Vecchio, J. (2006). Functional analysis and treatment of selective mutism in children. *The Journal of Speech-Language Pathology and Applied Behavior Analysis, 1*(2), 141+. Retrieved from http://www.questia.com

Kiecolt-Glaser, J. K., Belury, M. A., Andridge, R., Malarkey, W. B., & Glaser, R. (2011). Omega-3 supplementation lowers inflammation and anxiety in medical students: A randomized controlled trial. *Brain, Behavior, and Immunity, 25*(8), 1725-1734.

Kotta, I., & Szamosközi, S. (2012). Affective reactions to images in anxious children. *Journal of Evidence-Based Psychotherapies, 12*(1), 49+. Retrieved from http://www.questia.com

Leahy, R. L., & Holland, S. J. (2000). *Treatment plans and interventions for depression and anxiety disorders.* pp. 69-146. New York: Guilford Press.

Levy, F. J., Ranjbar, A., & Dean, C. H. (2006). Dance movement as a way to help children affected by war. *JOPERD--The Journal of Physical Education, Recreation & Dance, 77*(5), 6+. Retrieved from http://www.questia.com

Long, S., & Benton, D. (2013). Effects of vitamin and mineral supplementation on stress, mild psychiatric symptoms, and mood in nonclinical samples: A meta-analysis. *Psychosomatic Medicine, 75*(2), 144-153.

Martin, G., & Pear, J. (2003). *Behavior modification: What it is and how to do it.* pp. 339-352, 364, 372-373. Upper Saddle River, NJ: Prentice-Hall, Inc.

McLoone, J., Hudson, J. L., & Rapee, R. M. (2006). Treating anxiety disorders in a school setting. *Education & Treatment of Children, 29*(2), 219+. Retrieved from http://www.questia.com

McNamara, R. K., & Carlson, S. E. (2006). Role of omega-3 fatty acids in brain development and function: Potential implications for the pathogenesis and prevention of psychopathology. *Prostaglandins, Leukotrienes and Essential Fatty Acids, 75*(4-5), 329-349.

Miller, L. D., Short, C., Garland, E. J., & Clark, S. (2010). The ABCs of CBT (cognitive behavior therapy): Evidence-based approaches to child anxiety in public school settings. *Journal of Counseling and Development: JCD, 88*(4), 432+. Retrieved from http://www.questia.com

Morgan, H. (2006). Social distance: Self reports by black and white school age children. *Negro Educational Review, 57*(1/2), 15+. Retrieved from http://www.questia.com

Nhat Hahn, Thich. (2012). *A handful of quiet: Happiness in four pebbles.* Berkley, CA: Plum Blossom Books.

Olatunji, B. O., Cisler, J. M., & Deacon, B. J. (2010). Efficacy of cognitive behavioral therapy for anxiety disorders: A review of meta-analytic findings. *Psychiatric Clinics of North America, 33*(3), 19-32.

Orekoya, O. S., Chan, E. S. S., & Chik, M. P. Y. (2014). Humor and reading motivation in children: Does the tickling work? *Journal of Education, 6*(1), 61. Retrieved from http://www.questia.com

Orsillo, S. M., Roemer, L., Block-Lerner, J., & Tull, M. T. (2004). Acceptance, mindfulness, and cognitive-behavioral therapy: Comparisons, contrasts, and application to anxiety. In S. C. Hayes, M. M. Linehan, & V. M. Follette (Eds.), *Mindfulness, acceptance, and relationships: Expanding the cognitive-behavioral tradition* (pp. 66–95). New York: Guilford Publications, Inc.

Pitica, I., Susa, G., & Benga, O. (2010). The effects of attentional Training on attentional allocation to positive and negative stimuli in school-aged children: An explorative single case investigation. *Cognitie, Creier, Comportament, 14*(1), 63+. Retrieved from http://www.questia.com

Rachamim, L., Nacasch, N., Shafran, N., Tzur, D., & Gilboa-Schechtman, E. (2009). Exposure-based therapy for post-traumatic stress disorder in children and adults. *The Israel Journal of Psychiatry and Related Sciences, 46*(4), 274+. Retrieved from http://www.questia.com

Rajchanovska, D., & Zafirova, B. I. (2011). Prevalence of nail biting among preschool children in bitola. *The Journal of Special Education and Rehabilitation, 12*(1/2), 56+. Retrieved from http://www.questia.com

Rapee, R. M., Kennedy, S. J., Ingram, M., Edwards, S. L., & Sweeney, L. (2010). Altering the trajectory of anxiety in at-risk young children. *American Journal of Psychiatry, 167*. 1518-1525.

Reynolds, S., Wilson, C., Austin, J., & Hooper, L. (2012). Effects of psychotherapy for anxiety in children and adolescents: A meta-analytic review. *Clinical Psychology Review, 32*(4), 251-262.

Saint-Jacques, M., et al. (2006). The impact of serial transitions on behavioral and psychological problems among children in child protection services. *Child Welfare, 85*(6), 941+. Retrieved from http://www.questia.com

Sapolsky, R. M. (2004). *Why zebras don't get ulcers (3rd edition).* New York: Henry Holt and Company.

Schmidt, N. B., Lerew, D. R., & Trakowski, J. H. (1997). Body vigilance in panic disorder: Evaluating attention to bodily perturbations. *Journal of Consulting and Clinical Psychology, 65*, 214–220.

Semple, R., Reid, E., & Miller, L. (2005). Treating anxiety with mindfulness: An open trial of mindfulness training for anxious children. *Journal of Cognitive Psychotherapy, 19*(4), 379-392.